LEGACY COOKBOOK

A collection of secret family recipes from the friends of

CENTRAL BOSTON ELDER SERVICES

$29.95

Published by
Boston Common Press Limited Partnership
17 Station Street
Brookline, MA 02445

ISBN: 0-936184-99-X

Contents

Message from the Executive Director

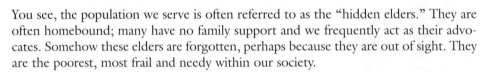

Four years ago, Central Boston Elder Services (CBES) launched its fundraising efforts by working with an event planner named Mark Oleszek. Each year, Mark and I would sit down and try to think of projects and themes that were creative and would help us get our message across about the very important home care services that CBES provides to 3,200 elders every year.

You see, the population we serve is often referred to as the "hidden elders." They are often homebound; many have no family support and we frequently act as their advocates. Somehow these elders are forgotten, perhaps because they are out of sight. They are the poorest, most frail and needy within our society.

Besides advocacy on their behalf, we often find our work involves protecting them from themselves or others. Our challenges have been to educate all involved and to bring the needs of this population to the forefront so that programs and services they rely on from our agency can receive additional funding support through individual donations.

Most of our programs lack adequate funding, yet we continue to provide vital services that allow elders to "age in place" within their communities for as long as possible. We also assist family members and caregivers. Our almost 30 years of experience has taught us that we cannot and should not rely upon state government to meet all of our funding needs. We realize that we must seek alternative sources for raising funds to support our elders and the services we provide.

Some of our past fundraising initiatives have included "The Picture of Aging," a project that brought together aspiring young artists from local art schools and the elderly of Boston. The project culminated in an exhibit that featured the elders as seen through the eyes of those young artists.

Another initiative was "Celebrating Centennial Elders," which featured a tribute to ten elders who reached 100 or more years of age and were still living in their own homes. Last year, our event paid tribute to seven physicians and the staff of a home care program that have continued the rare practice of "physician home visits."

This year's vision is the most ambitious and innovative so far: to capture in print the treasured recipes passed down through the generations. When I first heard the idea I thought, "What a great idea!" At that time none of us, including Mark, realized what a huge project and challenge we were about to take on.

Although the vision and idea were great ones, the problem we encountered was that many of these recipes had never been transcribed onto paper. Our lives are spent socializing and communicating with others around meals, yet we've often neglected to write down the recipes we hold dear. Most of the recipes were shared while standing in a kitchen over good conversation. A person would share a recipe by saying, "you need a little pinch of this and a little pinch of that." Consequently, many of these recipes are transcribed here for the first time.

One of the stories I heard during the preparation of this book was about a group of culturally diverse women who worked together in a factory during the "busing crisis," a dark time in Boston's history when there was great racial disharmony. These women bridged their ethnic and racial divides through the sharing of food and recipes. Ultimately, they became friends through the development of a recipe.

At CBES, we are rich in the diversity of our elder clients and staff. Each year, as an organization, we celebrate our rich cultures and diversity by coming together at our annual "International Potluck" luncheon. During the luncheon, the room is filled with the richness of food aromas, laughter, and artifacts from many cultures. Some of these "Potluck" recipes have also been included.

Part of the process of developing this cookbook was to gather and test the recipes. For the past year, we have solicited time-honored recipes from clients and friends for *The Legacy Cookbook*. This enabled us to broaden our educational efforts about the needs of our elders, while expanding and building upon our culturally diverse networks.

Along with the debut of our cookbook, we are pleased to recognize eleven well-known local restaurants with the presentation of our "Boston Legacy Award." This award is presented for their historical value and continued commitment to Boston and our community. Boston is fortunate to have so many restaurants that have survived the test of time.

This initiative would not have been possible without the work and support of many. I wish to thank our Board of Directors, staff, sponsors, chefs, restaurants, the *Boston Herald,* and Boston Common Press for all their support and contributions. I would like to thank Mark Oleszek especially, who has been a friend and supporter of CBES, and Michelle Carter, my Executive Assistant, both of whom played vital roles in bringing this book to fruition. Finally, I wish to thank the many cooks who shared their culture and heritage with us through their contributions to this book.

As is said in many cultures "God Bless the Cook." We hope that you will enjoy the cookbook and share it with friends and loved ones!

Catherine Hardaway, Executive Director

Message from the Board of Directors

This cookbook originated in the realization that Central Boston Elder Services (CBES) serves a wide variety of ethnic groups from every corner of the world. As such, our fundraising efforts should creatively reflect a means of sharing the various cultures represented by our clients, board, and staff.

The Board of Directors works closely with Catherine Hardaway, our Executive Director, to ensure that adequate resources are available not only to carry out our mission but also to seek ways in which we can increase services to elders while remaining within our budget. Although CBES is funded primarily by the Commonwealth of Massachusetts, many of our clients require additional funds for things most of us take for granted, such as meals, prescription drugs, and housing. This year, while faced with budget constraints from the state, CBES was able to deliver services to our clients through the efforts of an excellent management team, a prudent use of funds, and an active board.

The board wholeheartedly agreed that the sharing of favorite foods and recipes would promote an appreciation of our elderly and provide a means for bridging the gap between the culturally diverse young and old. Many dishes that are found in the various cultures around the world are very similar, differing primarily in the spices, herbs, and grains used in the preparation. Pasta, one of the original worldwide comfort foods, is a menu item that immediately comes to mind. All pasta is basically the same, yet every preparation is very different based on the region of the world in which the cook was born.

Throughout the years, the board has attempted different types of fundraising efforts to provide additional funding for CBES. This is the first project for which supporters receive a value beyond just writing a check. This cookbook would not exist if it were not for the efforts of Mark Oleszek. After reviewing the many recipes as well as conducting board and staff cook-offs to test the recipes, the cookbook was compiled based on an ongoing testing and evaluating process.

It is with great pleasure that I personally dedicate *The Legacy Cookbook* to the host of elders serviced by CBES. Don't let it sit on your bookshelf. Please try some of the recipes and let us know your opinion.

Perry C. Smith

Perry C. Smith, President, Board of Directors

The Legacy Cookbook

would not have been possible without the generous support of the following friends and corporations. We are grateful for their financial assistance on this ambitious project.

PATRON
Suburban Home Health Care, Inc.

SPONSOR
Massey & Co., LLC

CONTRIBUTORS
Blue Cross and Blue Shield of Massachusetts
Boston Public Library
Boston Magazine
Citizens Bank
Family Food Services, Inc.
State Street Bank and Trust Company
Verizon
Winthrop Laundry, Inc.

FRIENDS

1810 Realty Group, Inc.
Anodyne Homemaker Services Corporation
Beth Israel Deaconess Medical Center
Boston Aging Concerns–Young & Old United, Inc.
Boston Private Bank & Trust Company
Board of Boston Senior Home Care
Boston University Geriatric Services at
   Boston Medical Center
Ms. Thelma Callendar-Burns
Casner & Edwards, LLP
The CenterPoint Foundation, Inc.
City Fresh Foods
Mr. Alan Clarke
Commonwealth Co-operative Bank
Concord Communications, Inc.
The Cooperative Bank
Crittenton Hastings House
Daniel Dennis & Company, LLP
Epstein, Becker & Green, P.C.
Ethos
Federal Home Loan Bank of Boston
Speaker Thomas M. Finneran
Fleet Community Banking Group
Genesis ElderCare
Greater Boston Chinese Golden Age Center, Inc.

Hampshire House Corporation
HouseWorks, LLC
Huntington Markets
Jewish Community Housing for the Elderly
Jewish Family & Children's Service
Jewish Memorial Hospital and Rehabilitation Center
Kebadjian Jewelers
Lifeline Systems, Inc.
Maloney Properties, Inc.
Massachusetts Commission for Deaf and
   Hard of Hearing
MGH Senior HealthWISE
Midtown Home Health Services, Inc.
Mr. John Montgomery
Old Colony Elderly Services, Inc.
Peabody Resident Services, Inc.
Pioneer Medical Systems
Rainer, Walsh & O'Connor, LLP
Richardson & Associates
United South End Settlements
Urban Community Homemaker & Home
   Health Aide Service
Urban Medical Resources/Shopping Resources
The Waldwin Group, Inc., d/b/a Dunkin Donuts
Women's Educational and Industrial Union

Compiling *The Legacy Cookbook*

The idea for this ambitious fundraising project originated back in October 2000. I was coordinating another fundraising project honoring the many elders who had surpassed the all-important 100-year-old mark and were still living in their own homes with assistance provided by Central Boston Elder Services.

One of these honorees, Julia Carney, had lived on Shawmut Avenue in Boston's South End for all of her 106 years. In addition to being a devoted wife and mother, Mrs. Carney had volunteered her time by cooking for the entire parish at the former Fourth Methodist Church which was also located on Shawmut Avenue. She couldn't remember the exact amount of time she had cooked at the church, but guessed it was roughly 34 years. When Catherine Hardaway and I met with Mrs. Carney and asked about her cooking, her face lit up while she described all the great dishes she used to make for the crowds. Sadly, Mrs. Carney passed away last year, but her smile and enthusiasm provided the inspiration for this cookbook.

At a committee meeting held during the development of this project, someone mentioned, "You could write a book about this book!" Nothing could be closer to the truth. This journey has been tedious, eye-opening, all-consuming, frustrating, exciting, but most of all, rewarding. There are so many great memories in this book. It personally reminds me of those family get-togethers where there were always three or four dishes prepared by my mother, favorite aunt, or uncle that got my mouth watering in anticipation. Bringing the dish into the room and proudly placing it on the dining room table, they knew it would make everyone in the room happy. We couldn't wait until it was time to eat. This was a true passion for food.

I wish I had a dollar for every time I heard, "I wish I had written down my grand-mother's recipe for this or that!" We began *The Legacy Cookbook* to honor the last generation that learned how to prepare food without the use of microwave ovens or pre-made processed foods. That generation cooked these types of foods daily, which would be rare today when some people get overly anxious waiting more than two minutes for their supper. Many of these recipes take a lot of time to prepare but there is a great deal of pride and delight when tasting the finished product.

Many of the recipes were transcribed from memory. Some recipes were just scribbles on torn sheets of scrap

paper complete with egg, batter, or oil stains. Due to such vagaries, you can imagine the many mistakes made during testing. We held many "recipe testing" days to fine-tune the recipes and conducted these with the assistance of the staff at CBES, members of the American Institute of Wine & Food, and other friends and contributors. These were always educational and great fun for all involved, especially for those who had rarely cooked in the past.

One amusing reflection of this project is the story of a volunteer tester who was thumbing through recipes to test. She came across one that included ketchup as an ingredient. She stated emphatically that it was her understanding that there should be no processed foods in any of the recipes. I stated that we do indeed have a recipe for ketchup. To her great amazement, she asked, "They make ketchup from a recipe?"

Some recipes in this book include such old-time favorite ingredients as lard, salt pork, chicken fat, buttermilk, lots of butter, and other items that may not be construed today as being good for you. My philosophy on this matter is that 100 years ago it would have been unimaginable to sit down at one meal and eat a quarter pound of meat served on a sesame seed bun with a pound of fried potatoes on the side. Moderation is and always should be the key.

One more thing: To my taste, anything made with butter or sour cream always tastes better! In almost all cases, we tried to stay true to the original recipe. If you absolutely must prepare a dish using a substitute ingredient, it should work out fine since many of the recipes are flexible and forgiving. Please feel free to experiment.

For novice cooks, I strongly recommend reading or referencing *Julia's Kitchen Wisdom* by Julia Child, published by Alfred A. Knopf. This is an invaluable resource for understanding baking terms, techniques, and tricks of the trade. The book contains an excellent index and will clearly walk you through almost any technique that may seem foreign to someone just learning to cook. I am eternally grateful to Stephanie Hersh, Julia Child's personal assistant, for sending me a signed copy as a birthday present.

There are so many people to thank for helping to get this project get off the ground. We had a great team to collect and test the recipes. Christopher Kimball and Jim

McCormack of Boston Common Press, publishers of *The Legacy Cookbook*, were solidly behind this project from day one. Jane Dornbusch was instrumental in helping obtain recipes for a Mother's Day contest held in conjunction with the *Boston Herald*. I'm also indebted to our participating chefs and restaurateurs; the Boston chapter of the American Institute of Wine & Food; the staff, committee members, and board of directors at CBES; Rosemarie Peelle from Williams-Sonoma; Susan Davis from Barnes & Noble; Bernard Margolis and Jackie Hogan of the Boston Public Library; and the entire staff of Boston Common Press. In particular, I wish to extend my sincere gratitude to Jessica "Jess" Quirk of Boston Common Press for guiding me in all the right directions throughout this entire journey.

I also wish to thank everyone who buys this book! All proceeds will directly benefit clients of CBES. If you've ever had an elderly person in your family that required help or assistance in taking care of day-to-day needs, then you know how fortunate we are in Massachusetts to have a social service agency such as CBES.

I hope you cherish and utilize this small piece of history. Please feel free to contact me care of CBES if you have any suggestions or comments.

Cheers,

Mark Oleszek

Mark Oleszek

Committee members

Susan Able
Thelma Callendar-Burns
Michelle Carter
Genie Curry
Caleb DesRosiers
John Montgomery
Laura Morris
Primma-Latise Murry
Sephus Osborn
Rosemarie Peelle
James Poutre
Jessica Quirk

Recipe testing and fundraising team

Eleanor Arpino
Ron Bilodeau
Bradley Brown
Rosa Connolly
Renee Covalucci
Sherry Ellis
Nichelle Farrell
Sophia Glemaud
Shenelle Greene
M.J. Hakanson
Haris Hardaway
Michelle Hernandez

Natalia Itkins
Natalya Katalichenko
Irina Kogan
Pooi Seong Koong
Volf Kraytman
Teresa Lammey
Erin McMurrer
Anna Melnikova
Marina Minkin
Nikki Ndukwe
Frances O'Brien
Renee Parris-Brown

Joanne Peskowitz
Paul Richardson
Georgia Sharpe
Pat Skinner
Francine Smythwick
Jo Anne Vaughn
Jan Wall
Ada Yarbrough

And special thanks to:
Jon Bernier, graphic arts
Trish LaFleur, graphic arts
Ed McKinnon, photos

Breakfast & Breads

Wooden Shoes

Recipe donated by Cynthia E. Blain

❧ SERVES 4 TO 6

2 tablespoons butter
1 cup flour
¾ cup whole or 2 percent milk
½ teaspoon salt
3 large eggs
Butter (to taste)
Jam (to taste)

My mom made this fun and easy breakfast treat. The dish resembles a pair of wooden shoes and is similar to a popover when baked and puffed up. In the spring, my mom served this with homemade rhubarb sauce. To make the sauce, heat five cups of fresh rhubarb chunks, one cup water, and approximately one-half cup sugar; heat and reduce until mixture is syrupy. You may also serve this with crushed, sweet strawberries and whipped cream as a dessert. Take care when opening and closing the oven door so the Wooden Shoes don't fall.

1. Preheat oven to 425 degrees.

2. Melt butter in a 9-inch square baking pan, making sure to coat the bottom of the pan well.

3. Combine flour, milk, salt, and eggs in a medium-sized mixing bowl and mix well. Pour batter into the buttered baking pan.

4. Bake 20 minutes, or until top is golden brown and puffed. Remove from oven and serve warm with butter or jam.

Blueberry Muffins

Recipe donated by Dorsey B. Baron

~ MAKES 12 MUFFINS

1¾	cups flour
¾	cup sugar
2	teaspoons baking powder
¾	teaspoon salt
1	egg, slightly beaten
¾	cup milk
4	tablespoons butter, melted
1	cup fresh blueberries

1. Preheat oven to 425 degrees.

2. Combine flour, sugar, baking powder, and salt in a large mixing bowl. Add egg, milk, and melted butter; mix until smooth. Gently fold in blueberries.

3. Grease a standard-size muffin pan and fill with batter. Bake 15 minutes; remove from oven and cool 7 minutes. Loosen muffins and remove from pan. Serve warm.

Blueberry Sour Cream Coffeecake

This recipe was passed down to me from my mom, Sheila Reid, who inherited it from her cousin. It's moist and delicious and tastes best when you use fresh picked blueberries.

Recipe donated by Linda Flanagan

~❧ SERVES 8 TO 10

- 1¼ cups blueberries
- 1 teaspoon plus 2 cups flour
- ¼ pound butter, softened
- 1 cup sugar
- 2 large eggs
- 1 teaspoon baking soda
- 1 teaspoon baking powder
- 1 cup sour cream

Topping:

- ½ cup sugar
- 1 tablespoon cinnamon
- ¾ cup chopped walnuts or pecans

1. Preheat oven to 350 degrees.

2. Sprinkle blueberries with 1 teaspoon of flour and set aside. Prepare topping by combining ½ cup sugar, cinnamon, and chopped nuts in another small bowl and set aside.

3. Combine butter, 1 cup of sugar, and eggs in a large mixing bowl and mix until smooth. Add 2 cups of flour, baking soda, baking powder, and sour cream; mix well. Fold in blueberries.

4. Grease a 9- or 10-inch tube pan. Pour in half of the cake batter. Sprinkle half the cinnamon mixture on top. Fill the pan with the remaining batter and cover with the remaining cinnamon mixture. Gently swirl the batter with a knife to slightly mix the cinnamon mixture throughout the cake.

5. Bake for 45 to 50 minutes. Remove from oven and let cool before easing cake out of the pan.

Sitto's Walnut Coffeecake

Recipe donated by Alice Resha

SERVES 8 TO 10

2 cups sugar

4 eggs

½ pound butter, softened

2 teaspoons salt

2 teaspoons vanilla

1 cup milk

3 cups flour

1 cup chopped walnuts

Sitto is Arabic for grandmother. The one thing I remember most about making this coffeecake is that my sitto got everyone in the house to help out in the kitchen first thing in the morning. My brothers shelled and chopped the walnuts, and I helped make the coffeecake. The smell from the oven while this was baking was always unbelievable. This anticipation made the cake taste even better.

1. Preheat oven to 350 degrees.

2. Combine sugar, eggs, butter, salt, vanilla, and milk in a large mixing bowl; mix until smooth. Gradually mix in flour. Fold in walnuts.

3. Grease a 9-inch square baking pan or 11 by 7-inch pan. Pour in batter.

4. Bake approximately 55 minutes or until a toothpick inserted in the middle comes out clean. Remove from oven and let cool before serving.

Biscuit Cinnamon Rolls

Recipe donated by Hyacinth Singletary

SERVES 6 TO 8

Dough:

- 2 cups flour
- 3 teaspoons baking powder
- ⅓ cup sugar
- ½ teaspoon salt
- ½ cup vegetable oil
- ½ cup milk

Filling:

- 3 tablespoons cinnamon
- 1 teaspoon nutmeg
- ½ cup sugar
- ½ cup brown sugar
- 1 teaspoon vanilla
- ¾ cup raisins
- ¼ cup crushed walnuts or pecans (optional)
- ⅓ cup butter or margarine, melted
  Vanilla frosting (optional)

1. Preheat oven to 350 degrees.

2. Prepare dough by combining flour, baking powder, ⅓ cup sugar, salt, vegetable oil, and milk in a large mixing bowl; mix until smooth. Roll out dough to ¼ inch thickness on a lightly floured surface.

3. Combine cinnamon, nutmeg, ½ cup sugar, brown sugar, vanilla, raisins, and nuts, if desired, in a medium mixing bowl; mix well and set aside.

4. Brush ⅓ cup melted butter or margarine over the dough. Spread filling mixture over the dough to cover the entire surface.

5. Roll dough into a log. With a clean knife, gently slice roll into even pieces about 1½ inch thick.

6. Place rolled pieces in a lightly greased 9-inch round or square baking pan. Bake for approximately 30 minutes, or until light brown on top.

7. Allow to cool for a few minutes. Carefully loosen rolls from pan. Place a plate over the pan, invert, and tap out rolls. Drizzle tops of rolls with vanilla frosting or glaze if desired and serve warm.

Orange Nisu

Recipe donated by Margaret McKinney
SERVES 8 TO 10

- 1 cup warm milk, approximately 110 degrees
- 1 package yeast
- 1½ cups plus 4 cups flour
- 4 tablespoons butter, softened
- ½ cup sugar
- ½ teaspoon salt
- ½ teaspoon baking soda
  Grated rind and juice of 1 orange
- 2 eggs

This is an old Swedish recipe that smells heavenly while it's baking. You may be creative with the design of the loaves, opting to braid or form each individual section into one cloverleaf. You may also bake each loaf in a loaf pan. This tastes great plain or brushed with sugar and coffee topping or with confectioners' sugar and milk glaze.

1. Combine warm milk with one package of yeast in a small cup. Let sit until yeast dissolves and then combine with 1½ cups flour in a large mixing bowl to make a sponge. Knead well, then set aside for 30 minutes to let rise.

2. After 30 minutes, add butter, sugar, salt, baking soda, orange rind and juice, eggs, and 4 cups flour. Mix well and then knead. Cover with a cloth. Set aside to allow it to rise to approximately double the size.

3. Preheat oven to 375 degrees.

4. Divide dough into six equal sections. Roll out the six sections lengthwise on a flat work surface until each is one long strip. Braid three strips to form one loaf. Repeat braiding with the remaining three strips.

5. Place loaves on a rectangular baking sheet and bake for 20 to 25 minutes. Remove from oven to cool.

6. Serve plain or brushed with a mixture of ½ cup sugar and ½ cup cold coffee, or top with a glaze of 2 cups confectioners' sugar and 1 cup milk.

Swiss Eggs

Recipe donated by Esme Littleton
SERVES 4

- 1 ounce butter, softened, plus 1 tablespoon butter, melted
- 3 ounces Swiss or cheddar cheese, thinly sliced, plus 1 ounce Swiss or cheddar cheese, grated
- 4 eggs
- 2 tablespoons heavy cream
- Salt and pepper to taste

1. Preheat oven to 375 degrees.

2. Place small pats of butter over the bottom of an 11 by 7-inch or 9-inch square baking pan then cover with cheese slices.

3. Carefully crack each egg over the cheese slices, spacing them evenly and taking care not to break the yolks. Pour ½ tablespoon of cream over each egg. Season to taste with salt and pepper. Sprinkle grated cheese evenly over eggs.

4. Bake for 7 to 10 minutes, or until eggs are set soft. Just before serving, place dish one inch under the broiler for one minute, basting every few seconds with a little melted butter. Serve while hot.

Eggs Borghese

Recipe donated by Herta Carlson

❧ SERVES 4

        2 tablespoons butter
        1 onion slice, ¼ inch thick
     1½ cups tomato sauce
     1½ cups water
       ½ teaspoon salt
       ½ teaspoon pepper
       ½ teaspoon nutmeg
        4 eggs, hardboiled, peeled, and quartered

1. Melt butter in a medium skillet over medium high heat. Add onion and sauté until golden brown.

2. Add tomato sauce, water, salt, pepper, and nutmeg; stir well. Reduce heat to medium low and cook for 20 minutes.

3. Add egg quarters to sauce in skillet. Carefully stir in eggs and simmer for an additional two minutes. Serve while hot.

New Orleans French Toast

Recipe donated by Cynthia E. Blain
SERVES 6 TO 8

8	eggs, beaten
1½	cups half and half
2	tablespoons plus ¾ cup light brown sugar
½	teaspoon salt
2	teaspoons vanilla
8	slices French bread, sliced thick
½	cup butter
½	cup maple syrup
¾	cup pecans, chopped

1. Combine beaten eggs, half and half, 2 tablespoons brown sugar, salt, and vanilla in a medium mixing bowl; mix well.

2. Pour half of this mixture into a 9 by 13-inch pan. Cover with bread slices. Top with remaining egg mixture. Cover and refrigerate for at least 4 hours or overnight.

3. Preheat oven to 350 degrees.

4. Melt butter in a second 9 by 13-inch pan, then stir in ¾ cup brown sugar, maple syrup, and pecans. Top with egg-soaked bread slices.

5. Bake for 30 to 35 minutes, or until bread slices are brown and puffed.

6. To serve, cut into squares and top with additional maple syrup if desired.

Eggs in a Nest

Recipe donated by Jim Poutre
SERVES 4

- 1 tablespoon butter
- 4 slices bread
- 4 eggs, separated
- 8 slices bacon

1. Preheat oven to 375 degrees.

2. Butter one side of each bread slice. Place bread slices, butter side down, in an ungreased 9 by 13-inch baking pan.

3. Beat egg whites to stiff peaks. Spoon egg whites evenly over bread slices. Make a gully in the center of each bread slice. Carefully place an egg yolk in each gully.

4. Place 2 strips of bacon over the egg whites on each bread slice, making sure an egg yolk pokes through the strips.

5. Bake for 25 to 30 minutes or until bacon is done.

Thin Polish Pancakes

Recipe donated by Louise Kinoske

❧ MAKES APPROXIMATELY 24 SMALL PANCAKES

This recipe has been in our family for many years. It makes a quick and easy breakfast treat. The pancakes taste best with just a bit of sugar or maple syrup on top; no additional butter is necessary.

2	eggs
2	cups flour
1	teaspoon baking powder
1½	teaspoons salt
1½	cups milk
4	tablespoons vegetable oil

1. Combine eggs, flour, baking powder, salt, and milk in a large mixing bowl. Whisk until pancake batter is smooth and creamy. Add additional milk if batter seems lumpy.

2. Heat 2 tablespoons vegetable oil in a large skillet over high heat. Lower heat to medium and slowly ladle approximately ¼ cup batter onto the pan for each pancake, up to 3 pancakes at one time. Flip once the edges start to brown. Fry until both sides are lightly brown around the edges, but still egg colored in the middle.

3. Repeat until all batter is used, adding vegetable oil to the skillet as needed. Pancakes may be stored on a plate in a warm oven until ready.

4. Serve with sugar, maple syrup, or an assortment of fresh berries or fruit.

Grandma's Oatmeal Bread

Recipe donated by Francine and John Hauck

SERVES 8

2	packages dry yeast
½	cup warm water plus 1½ cups boiling water
1	cup rolled oats
½	cup molasses
1	tablespoon salt
⅓	cup vegetable shortening
5½–6	cups flour, sifted
2	eggs, lightly beaten
1	teaspoon vegetable oil

1. Combine yeast and ½ cup warm water in a small bowl. Set aside to let soften.

2. Combine 1½ cups boiling water, rolled oats, molasses, salt, and vegetable shortening in a large mixing bowl. Stir then let cool to lukewarm. Stir in 2 cups flour and eggs; beat well. Stir in softened yeast; beat well. Add remaining flour and stir to make a soft dough. Dough will be a bit sticky. Grease top of dough lightly with vegetable oil. Cover tightly and refrigerate for at least 2 hours or overnight.

3. Divide and shape dough into 2 equal loaves. Place loaves into 2 greased 9-inch loaf pans. Cover with a clean towel and set pans in a warm place to let loaves rise and double in size, about 2 hours.

4. Preheat oven to 375 degrees.

5. Bake for 40 to 50 minutes. Remove loaves from oven and set aside to cool before tapping out of pans.

Julia's Irish Bread

Recipe donated by Judy Breen

~ SERVES 10 TO 12

    1   cup plus 2 tablespoons sugar
    ½   cup butter, melted
    1   egg
    1   teaspoon vanilla
    2   teaspoons baking powder
    2   cups flour
    ¼   cup whole milk
    ¾   cup raisins
    2   teaspoons caraway seeds

Sister Judy Breen, C.S.J., shares her mother's prized Irish Bread recipe with Sean Newell of M. J. O'Connor's restaurant in Boston's Back Bay. Sister Breen, who was born in the South End, has kept this recipe a secret all these years. She notes, "I'm not sure if my mother would approve, but it's nice to share this special memory with so many people."

1. Preheat oven to 350 degrees.

2. Combine sugar and melted butter in a medium mixing bowl.

3. Add the egg, vanilla, baking powder, and flour; mix until creamy.

4. Slowly add milk until the batter is moist, but thick. Fold in raisins and caraway seeds.

5. Lightly grease the inside bottom and sides of an 8-inch round pan with butter. Sprinkle flour into the pan and shake to completely cover the surface. Turn pan upside down and bang out all excess flour.

6. Pour the batter into the pan. Sprinkle 2 tablespoons of sugar on top.

7. Bake for 45 minutes. Allow to cool before tapping out of pan to serve.

Durgin Park's Corn Bread

Recipe donated by Seana Kelley-Chase
~ MAKES ABOUT 18 PIECES

¾ cup sugar

2 eggs, lightly beaten

2 cups flour

¾ teaspoon salt

1 tablespoon baking powder

1 cup granulated yellow cornmeal

1½ tablespoons butter, melted

1½ cups milk

This basic recipe has been made at Durgin Park since before anyone can remember. You can experiment by adding just about anything in one cup portions—blueberries, cranberries, or even chopped jalapeño peppers.

1. Preheat oven to 375 degrees.

2. Combine sugar and beaten eggs in a large mixing bowl. Sift together flour, salt, and baking powder; add with cornmeal to the egg mixture and mix well. Add melted butter and milk and combine thoroughly.

3. Grease a 9 by 13-inch baking dish. Pour in batter and bake for approximately 25 to 30 minutes.

4. Allow to cool a few minutes. Cut into squares and serve.

Starters

Stuffed Grape Leaves with Lamb

Recipe donated by Nellie David

∼ SERVES 10 TO 12

- 1 pound grapevine leaves, young fresh or preserved
- 1 cup white rice
- 1½ pounds ground lamb or ground beef
- 1 teaspoon dried mint
- 1 teaspoon plus 3 tablespoons salt for boiling
- 1 teaspoon pepper
- Juice of 2 lemons, approximately ½ to ¾ cup

1. Remove stems from fresh or preserved grape leaves and wash. Fill a medium stockpot with salted water and bring to a boil. Blanch fresh leaves in boiling water for approximately 30 seconds or preserved leaves for approximately 1 minute. Remove leaves from water and set on paper towels to dry.

2. Wash rice in cold water until water runs clear. Combine rice, meat, mint, 1 teaspoon salt, and pepper in a large mixing bowl.

3. Arrange 1 leaf under-side up and place approximately ½ tablespoon of the filling across the stem end. Turn the stem end up and fold over the sides, rolling tightly to form a cigar shape. Repeat process with additional leaves until all filling is used.

4. Line the bottom of a medium-sized stockpot with broken and torn leaves to prevent scorching. Pack one layer of stuffed grape leaves tightly in the stock-pot. Salt generously, then add a second layer. Repeat until all stuffed grape leaves are used.

5. Add water to the stockpot until leaves are covered. Invert a plate over the rolls to hold them tightly in place.

6. Bring the water to a boil, then lower heat, simmering until rice is cooked through, approximately 30 minutes.

7. Add lemon juice near the end of the cooking time so the flavor will not boil off. Serve hot or chilled with plain yogurt.

Squid Salad

Recipe donated by Elena Arpino
SERVES 8 TO 10

       2 pounds squid, cleaned and cut into ¼-inch slices
      ½ cup chopped fresh parsley
          Salt and pepper to taste
       1 cup chopped celery
       1 cup sliced black olives
       1 cup chopped red (Italian) onion
       2 cloves garlic, finely chopped
      ½ teaspoon fresh oregano
      ½ cup extra virgin olive oil
       2 tablespoons lemon juice

1. Place squid in a dry, large skillet and cook over medium heat, stirring frequently. Add fresh parsley and salt and pepper to taste while cooking.

2. When squid is cooked through, approximately 5 minutes, drain squid juices from the pan and set aside to cool.

3. Combine celery, olives, onion, garlic, and oregano in a large mixing or serving bowl.

4. When squid is cool, add to the bowl and toss with olive oil and lemon juice.

5. Season with salt and pepper to taste. Serve chilled or at room temperature.

Stuffed Grape Leaves with Vegetable Tabbouleh

Recipe donated by Nellie David

❧ SERVES 10 TO 12

1 cup fine burghul (cracked wheat)

1 pound grapevine leaves, young fresh or preserved

1 bunch scallions or 1 onion, finely chopped

2 large bunches fresh parsley, finely chopped

½ bunch of fresh mint, finely chopped, or 1 tablespoon dry mint

2 medium tomatoes, finely chopped

½ cup olive oil

1 clove garlic, finely chopped

1 teaspoon plus 3 tablespoons salt for boiling

1 teaspoon pepper

Juice of 2 lemons, about ½ to ¾ cup

1. Soak burghul in cold water in a medium mixing bowl for 30 minutes.

2. Remove stems from fresh or preserved grape leaves and wash leaves. Fill a medium stockpot with salted water and bring to a boil. Blanch fresh leaves in boiling water for approximately 30 seconds or preserved leaves for approximately 1 minute. Remove from water and set aside on paper towels to dry.

3. Combine scallions or onions, parsley, mint, tomatoes, olive oil, garlic, salt, and pepper in a large mixing bowl. Drain burghul, add to bowl, and mix well.

4. Arrange one leaf under-side up and place approximately ½ tablespoon of the filling across the stem end. Turn stem end up and fold over the sides, rolling tightly to form a cigar shape. Repeat process until all filling is used.

5. Line the bottom of a medium-sized stockpot with broken and torn leaves to prevent scorching. Pack one layer of stuffed grape leaves tightly in the stockpot. Salt generously, then add a second layer. Repeat until all stuffed grape leaves are used.

6. Add water to the stockpot until leaves are covered. Invert a plate over the rolls to hold them tightly in place.

7. Bring the water to a boil, then lower heat and simmer for approximately 30 minutes.

8. Add lemon juice towards the end of the cooking time so the flavor will not boil off. Serve chilled with plain yogurt.

House Cured Salmon

Recipe donated by Ray Gardiner

✎ SERVES 10 TO 12

- 1 bunch fresh dill, finely chopped
- ½ pound rock or kosher salt
- 1½ pounds sugar
- 3 pound boneless salmon fillet, skin on
- ¼ cup vodka
- 1 teaspoon fresh-ground black pepper
- 2 limes, zest only

While working as executive chef at M.J. O'Connor's in Boston's Back Bay, Ray Gardiner developed several recipes, some in this book, that originated from his grandmother in their native Ireland. Ray has since moved on to start his own restaurant, Cu Na Mara, located in Bristol, New Hampshire.

1. Make the cure by mixing the dill, salt, and sugar in a large bowl.

2. Cut 2 pieces of plastic kitchen wrap, approximately 30-inches long each. Overlap sheets to make one sheet. Place wrap flat on a hard work surface.

3. Place ¼ of the dill, salt, and sugar mixture on the plastic sheet, approximately 1 inch thick at one end and decreasing to ¼ inch thick at the other end. Place salmon, skin side down, on top of the cure, with the head on the 1-inch thick end.

4. Cover the top of the salmon with the rest of the cure.

5. Wrap the salmon tightly with the plastic wrap and place on a sheet pan. Cover with another sheet pan, then place 6 heavy cans or weights on top. Place in a cool, dry place and press for 48 to 72 hours.

6. Once the salmon is cured, remove the plastic wrap and rinse with plenty of cold water.

7. Place the salmon skin side down and hand rub the vodka, black pepper, and lime zest directly into the flesh. Place in refrigerator, uncovered, until dry.

Eggplant Sauté

Recipe donated by Sofia Simkina
SERVES 6

- 2 medium-sized eggplants, halved
- 3 red peppers, halved and seeded
- 4 tomatoes
- 3 cloves garlic
- 1 tablespoon sugar
- 2 tablespoons vinegar
- 3 tablespoons olive oil
  Salt and ground pepper to taste

1. Preheat oven to 350 degrees.

2. Place eggplant halves and red peppers cut sides down in a rectangular baking pan with a little water to cover the bottom of the pan. Bake for approximately 35 minutes, or until eggplant and peppers are soft. Remove from oven and set aside to cool.

3. Place tomatoes in a medium saucepan with water to cover. Bring to boil over high heat. Set aside to cool.

4. Peel the eggplant and tomatoes when cool. Cut eggplant, tomatoes, and red peppers into 1-inch chunks.

5. Place eggplant, tomatoes, red peppers, and garlic into a food processor and mix until well blended, but not pureed.

6. Mix in sugar, vinegar, olive oil, and salt and pepper to taste. Cover and chill.

7. Serve chilled or at room temperature with toast points or crackers.

Homemade Ketchup

Recipe donated by Ruth Austin
~ MAKES APPROXIMATELY 2 QUARTS

    4 quarts ripe tomatoes, peeled and seeded
    2 medium onions, peeled and finely chopped
    3 red peppers, seeded and sliced thin
    1 tablespoon whole allspice
    1 tablespoon cloves
    1 stick cinnamon
  ⅓ cup sugar
    2 teaspoons celery salt
    2 tablespoons salt
    2 teaspoons dry mustard
    1 teaspoon paprika
    2 cups vinegar

1. Combine tomatoes, onions, and red peppers in a large stockpot. Do not add water. Heat slowly over low heat until soft. Place a fine strainer over a large, 4-quart pot and press tomatoes, onions, and peppers through the strainer.

2. Make a small pocket out of cheesecloth and place allspice, cloves, and cinnamon stick inside. Tie with string at the top and place into pot with tomato pulp.

3. Add sugar, celery salt, salt, dry mustard, and paprika to the tomato pulp. Stir and bring to a boil over high heat. Reduce heat to medium and simmer rapidly for one hour.

4. Add vinegar and continue cooking until mixture is thick.

5. Remove cheesecloth bag and pour hot ketchup into sterilized individual containers and seal. Refrigerate after opening.

Casa Romero's Casera Sauce

Recipe donated by Leo Romero
MAKES 2 CUPS

2	tomatoes, finely chopped
1	onion, chopped
1	clove garlic, finely chopped
1–2	jalapeño peppers, seeded and finely chopped
1	tablespoon fresh chopped cilantro
1	tablespoon lemon juice
1½	teaspoons vegetable oil
½	teaspoon oregano

1. Combine tomatoes, onion, garlic, jalapeño peppers, cilantro, lemon juice, oil, and oregano in a medium mixing bowl; mix well.

2. Cover and refrigerate for at least 4 hours. Serve as an appetizer with tortilla chips.

Vidalia Viennoise

Recipe donated by Hannelore Manifold
~~ SERVES 4 TO 6

- 1 large Vidalia onion, peeled and sliced
- 1 cup mayonnaise
- 1 cup Parmesan cheese,
  freshly sliced, not grated

Garnish:
- 1 tablespoon chopped fresh parsley (optional)
- ½ teaspoon paprika (optional)
- Melba toast or a crusty French baguette

I first learned about this recipe many years ago from my aunt who raised me in my native Austria. When I moved to the United States, I began using Vidalia onions and renamed the dish, Vidalia Viennoise. This is easy to prepare, delicious, and will have everyone guessing about the ingredients.

1. Preheat oven to 350 degrees.

2. Combine Vidalia onion slices, mayonnaise, and Parmesan cheese in a medium mixing bowl; mix until ingredients are thoroughly combined.

3. Place mixture in a medium-sized casserole dish and bake for 30 minutes or until top is lightly browned.

4. Sprinkle lightly with either parsley or paprika. Serve with Melba toast for dipping or in individual portions with sliced French baguette as an appetizer.

Mom's Chinese Egg Rolls

Recipe donated by Ann Marie Franklin
🍲 MAKES ABOUT 4 DOZEN

4–4½   pounds Chinese sausage
   4   cups bean sprouts
   2   large carrots, peeled and shredded
   1   medium green cabbage, shredded
   8   scallions, chopped
   ¾   cup water chestnuts, finely chopped
   ⅛   teaspoon freshly ground ginger
   3   tablespoons soy sauce
   1   teaspoon minced garlic
   ⅓   cup cooking wine or sherry
   1   teaspoon salt
 5–6   cups vegetable shortening
   4   dozen egg roll wraps
   2   cups sweet and sour sauce

1. Remove sausage from skins. Break meat apart into small pieces and place in a large saucepan. Cook over medium heat until sausage is cooked through.

2. Add bean sprouts, carrots, cabbage, scallions, water chestnuts, ginger, soy sauce, garlic, cooking wine, and salt. Stir frequently until cabbage shrinks, approximately 20 minutes. Reduce heat to low and simmer for 40 minutes. Remove from heat and drain in strainer. Set aside to cool.

3. Heat shortening in a large saucepan over high heat.

4. Place approximately eight egg roll wraps at a time on a flat, clean work surface. Place approximately 2 tablespoons of stuffing at the bottom of each wrap. Fold in sides and roll-up into cigar shapes.

5. Test the shortening temperature by dropping in a small corner of an egg roll wrap; it should rise quickly. Drop 3 to 4 egg rolls at a time into the hot shortening. Cook, turning until all sides are an even golden brown. Remove with a slotted spoon and set on paper towels to drain.

6. Serve while warm with sweet and sour sauce.

Pastieie

Recipe donated by Dorothy B. Costa
SERVES 12

1	pound elbow macaroni
½	teaspoon vegetable or olive oil
12	eggs
2	cups ricotta cheese
½	cup grated Romano cheese
½	cup shredded cheddar cheese
½	cup shredded mozzarella cheese
2	large sticks pepperoni, cut into small pieces
1	teaspoon black pepper
1	teaspoon salt

1. Cook elbow macaroni according to instructions on package. Drain and place in a large mixing bowl. Toss with oil and set aside to cool.

2. Preheat oven to 350 degrees.

3. Beat eggs in a separate, large mixing bowl, then combine with cooled macaroni. Add ricotta, Romano, cheddar, mozzarella, pepperoni, pepper, and salt; toss until well mixed.

4. Pour mixture into a greased 9 by 13-inch baking pan. Make sure all noodles are covered with cheese and egg mixture. Bake for 1 hour, or until golden on top. Remove from oven and allow to cool.

5. Cut into sections approximately 3-inches by 1-inch and serve as an appetizer. Sprinkle with additional salt and pepper to taste. May also be refrigerated and served chilled.

Marinated Mushrooms

Recipe donated by Barbara Cedrone Horan
  SERVES 4

- 1 cup olive or vegetable oil
- 1 clove garlic, sliced in half
- 1 pound fresh mushrooms, sliced
- 2 tablespoons vinegar
- 2 tablespoons fresh lemon juice
- 1 teaspoon salt
- ⅛ teaspoon black pepper

1. Heat oil in a heavy skillet over medium heat. Add garlic and cook until it browns slightly, approximately 2 minutes. Add mushrooms and cook just until they begin to darken, approximately 5 minutes.

2. Add vinegar, lemon juice, salt, and pepper. Reduce heat to low and simmer for approximately 10 minutes.

3. Place in a crockery container with a tight lid and refrigerate for at least 4 hours.

Salmon Salad with Lemon Ginger Dressing

Recipe donated by Connie Emerson

SERVES 4

Lemon Ginger Dressing:

¼ cup fresh lemon juice

1 cup honey

1 8-ounce brick cream cheese, softened

½ cup lemon-lime soft drink

½ teaspoon fresh ginger, finely chopped

1 pound salmon fillet, cooked

8 Boston lettuce leaves

1 cup fresh strawberries, halved

1 cup fresh blueberries

1 avocado, peeled and sliced

1. Chill four salad plates.

2. Make dressing by combining lemon juice, honey, cream cheese, lemon-lime soft drink, and ginger in a blender; pulse for approximately 1 minute.

3. Cut salmon fillet into bite sized pieces. Set aside.

4. Place two Boston lettuce leaves on each chilled plate. Top with salmon, strawberries, blueberries, and avocado slices.

5. Drizzle Lemon Ginger dressing over each salad and serve.

Union Oyster House Scalloped Oysters

Recipe donated by Bill Coyne

SERVES 6

12 oysters, freshly shucked

¼ cup seasoned bread crumbs

Sauce:

½ ounce butter

1 teaspoon garlic, chopped

1 ounce white wine

8 ounces heavy cream

½ teaspoon Dijon mustard

⅛ teaspoon thyme, dried

Salt and pepper to taste

1. Remove oysters from shells and set aside. Save bottom shells.

2. Make sauce in a medium-sized saucepan by melting butter over medium high heat. Add garlic and sauté until sizzling; add wine to deglaze the pan. Mix in cream, Dijon mustard, thyme, and salt and pepper to taste. Stir occasionally until sauce is thick and reduced by half.

3. Preheat oven to 450 degrees.

4. Place the reserved bottom shells on a broiler or baking pan. Line each shell with approximately ½ teaspoon seasoned bread crumbs, topped with 1 teaspoon sauce. Place an oyster on each shell and cover with the rest of the sauce.

5. Broil oysters for 3 to 5 minutes, or until they are brown and bubbly. Remove from oven and allow to cool a few minutes before serving.

Scalloped Oysters Casserole

Recipe donated by Dorsey B. Baron
~& SERVES 6

- 1 pint oysters with juice
- ½ cup dry breadcrumbs
- 1 cup cracker crumbs
- ½ cup butter, melted
- 2 tablespoons heavy cream
- 2 tablespoons dry sherry
- ¼ teaspoon salt
- ¼ teaspoon pepper
- ¼ teaspoon nutmeg

1. Preheat oven to 450 degrees.

2. Drain oysters and reserve juice; set aside.

3. Combine dry breadcrumbs, cracker crumbs, and melted butter in a medium mixing bowl; set aside.

4. Combine 2 tablespoons reserved juice from oysters, heavy cream, and sherry in a small mixing bowl; mix and set aside.

5. Line the bottom of a shallow, greased 2-quart casserole or baking dish with a thin layer of the breadcrumb mixture. Layer the oysters on top, then sprinkle with salt, pepper, and nutmeg. Drizzle half the cream and sherry mixture over, top with another layer of the breadcrumb mixture, then repeat the process. Finish with a layer of the breadcrumb mixture on top.

6. Bake for 30 minutes. Allow to cool for a few minutes before serving.

Potato Latkes

Recipe donated by Sarah Markovich

❧ SERVES 4

- 5 potatoes, peeled and coarsely grated
- 2 eggs
- 2 medium onions, peeled and finely grated
- 3 tablespoons matzoh meal
- ½ teaspoon baking soda
- 1 tablespoon kosher salt
- ¼ teaspoon white pepper
- 1 cup vegetable or olive oil

Optional toppings:

- ½ cup sour cream
- ½ cup apple sauce, apple chutney, or fruit compote

There are many variations of potato pancakes or latkes throughout the world, but it wasn't until the early 18th century that potatoes were grown in central Europe by order of Prussia's Frederick II. Going back two thousand years to the ancient city of Jerusalem and the origin of Hanukkah, latkes were reserved for celebrations since they were fried in oil. This is related to the story of the discovery of oil in the destroyed temple that was expected to last only one night but that kept the lamps lit for 8 days.

1. Peel potatoes and keep in a cool water bath. Grate either by hand or in a food processor.

2. Beat eggs in a large mixing bowl. Add grated potatoes, onions, matzoh meal, baking soda, salt, and pepper; stir until combined.

3. Heat ½ cup vegetable or olive oil in a large skillet over high heat. Lower heat to medium and slowly ladle approximately ½ cup batter for each latke (you should be able to fit 3 latkes) onto the fry pan. Be careful of spattering oil. Fry and flip until both sides are golden brown. When done, remove from the skillet and drain on paper towels.

4. Repeat until all batter is used, adding oil to the skillet as needed. Latkes may be stored in a warm oven until ready to serve.

5. Fan three to four latkes on a medium sized plate. Serve plain or with sour cream and apple chutney or fruit compote.

Pierogi with Sauerkraut or Potato Filling

Recipe donated by Casimir Szmaj
SERVES 6 TO 8

Dough:

- 2 cups flour
- 1 teaspoon salt
- 2 tablespoons butter, softened
- 1 egg
- ½ cup very warm water

Sauerkraut Filling:

- 4 cups sauerkraut (32-ounce can)
- ¼ cup vegetable oil
- 1 large onion, chopped
- ½ cup sliced mushrooms
- ½ teaspoon salt
- ½ teaspoon pepper

Potato Filling:

- 2 pounds potato, peeled, cooked, and mashed
- ¼ pound cheddar cheese, shredded
- ½ teaspoon salt
- ½ teaspoon pepper

1. Make dough by sifting flour and salt into a mixing bowl. Add butter, egg, and warm water; mix well and knead until the dough is smooth. Turn the dough out onto a floured work surface. Roll dough out with a rolling pin until it is ¼ inch thick.

2. Drain and rinse sauerkraut and set aside.

3. Make sauerkraut filling by heating oil in a large skillet over low heat. Add onion and mushrooms; cook until soft. Add sauerkraut, salt, and pepper; cook until tender. Set aside to cool.

4. Make potato filling by mixing potatoes, cheese, salt, and pepper in a large mixing bowl; set aside to cool.

5. Cut the dough into rounds with the rim of a 3-inch drinking glass or cookie cutter. Place 1 teaspoon filling in the middle of each dough round. Fold circles into half moons; seal tightly by pressing with fingers or with the tines of a fork.

6. Bring approximately 2 quarts of water to a boil in a large stockpot over high heat. Lower heat to simmer, then place pierogi into the water. Cover and cook until the pierogi float to the top, approximately 3 minutes.

7. Serve hot. May be served plain, with sautéed onions, or with drawn butter with breadcrumbs.

Piroshki Stuffed with Cabbage

Recipe donated by Margarita Dobrushkina

~ SERVES 6 TO 8

Dough:

- 2 tablespoons vinegar
- 2 tablespoons olive oil
- 1 egg
- ½ teaspoon salt
- 1 cup water
- 1 cup butter, softened
- 2 cups flour

Stuffing:

- 1 head green cabbage, finely shredded
- 3 tablespoons butter
- 3 tablespoons olive oil
- 3 eggs, hard-boiled, chopped
- 2 tablespoons fresh dill, finely chopped
- ½ teaspoon salt
- ½ teaspoon pepper
- 1 cup sour cream (optional)

1. Make the dough in large bowl by combining vinegar, olive oil, 1 egg, salt, and water; mix well. Add butter and flour and hand knead into a soft dough that does not stick to your fingers. Cut dough in half, wrap with a towel, and refrigerate.

2. Make the stuffing by blanching the cabbage in boiling salted water in a stockpot for 3 minutes. Drain cabbage and cool for a few minutes. Squeeze out excess liquid with paper towels and set aside.

3. Heat butter and olive oil in a medium-sized skillet over medium heat. Add cabbage, stir, and cook for 20 minutes. Remove from the heat. Add chopped, hard-boiled eggs, fresh dill, salt, and pepper and set aside to cool.

Piroshki, as they are called in Russia, or Pierogi, as they are called in Poland, were always served at weddings, Christmas, birthdays, and special events. There are many variations for the stuffing based on local meats, fish, fruits, or vegetables readily available in the area. To make a Polish dessert version, use the recipe for Cheese Pierogi on page 256.

4. Remove dough from the refrigerator and roll each half into a very thin circle on a hard work surface. This takes some effort as the dough springs back. Once the dough half is in an even circle, use a 3-inch round cookie cutter or the rim of a drinking glass to cut into circles.

5. Place a small spoonful of cabbage filling in the middle of each circle and fold it over so it makes a half moon. Press the edges of the half moons together with your fingers, and seal with sprinkles of cold water from your fingertips.

6. Preheat oven to 350 degrees.

7. Place the filled half moons on an ungreased baking sheet and bake for 15 minutes. Serve hot, as is, or with a tablespoon of sour cream on top.

Potato Dumplings with Bacon

Recipe donated by Greg Oleszek
SERVES 6

- 2 pounds potatoes, peeled and grated
- 1 cup flour
- 2 eggs, lightly beaten
- ½ teaspoon plus 1 teaspoon salt
- ¼ teaspoon pepper
- 1 pound thick bacon
- 1 onion, peeled and sliced

1. Press grated potatoes in a clean white cloth to squeeze out excess moisture.

2. Combine grated potatoes, flour, eggs, ½ teaspoon salt, and pepper in a large mixing bowl; mix well and set aside.

3. Bring 2 quarts water and 1 teaspoon salt to a boil in a large stockpot over medium heat. Gently roll 1 teaspoon batter in your palm with your index finger to form a small cigar shape. Drop the rolled batter into the boiling water. Repeat this process quickly until all batter is used. Cover and boil dumplings until each rises to the top. Remove dumplings with a slotted spoon, drain, and set aside.

4. Fry the bacon in a large skillet over medium heat. Do not allow the bacon to become too crispy. Remove bacon slices and set aside on paper towels to drain and cool. When all bacon is fried, retain half the bacon fat in the skillet and save the rest in a small bowl. Add onion to the skillet and sauté for approximately 10 minutes over medium heat.

5. Crumple or cut bacon up into small pieces when cool.

6. Carefully add approximately 2 cups dumplings to the skillet when the onions are just about tender. Add some of the bacon and lightly fry in batches until all dumplings and bacon are lightly sautéed in the bacon fat. Use additional bacon fat when needed. Serve while hot.

Aunt Harriet's Carrot Marmalade

Recipe donated by Terence Janericco
~~ MAKES 6 PINTS

- 4 pounds carrots, peeled, ends cut off, cut into ⅛-inch slices
- 2 cups water
- 6 small lemons, unpeeled, ends cut off
- 7 cups sugar

1. Place carrots in a medium stockpot and add 1½ cups water or just enough to cover. Cover and cook over low heat for 1 hour.

2. Cut lemons into pieces, leaving the peel on. Remove all seeds and grind the lemons finely with a hand mixer or in a food processor. Combine lemons and ½ cup water in a medium saucepan. Cook over very low heat for 1 hour. Stir occasionally, checking for scorching regularly.

3. Add the lemons to the carrots in the stockpot. Stir in the sugar. Simmer over lowest heat for 6 hours, stirring often and checking regularly for burning. Beware: the marmalade can burn easily.

4. Marmalade is ready when a tablespoon is left to cool on a small plate and sets to jam consistency.

5. While hot, spoon marmalade into sterilized jars. Cover loosely, allow to cool for at least 3 hours, then tighten lids. Store in a cool, dry place or refrigerate.

Red Onion, Port, and Apple Marmalade

Recipe donated by Ray Gardiner
MAKES 4 CUPS

3	tablespoons olive oil
2	red onions, peeled and sliced
1½	cups port wine
1½	cups red wine
2	apples, peeled, cored, and sliced ½ inch thick
2	teaspoons raspberry jam
½	cup chicken or vegetable broth
¼	bunch fresh oregano, chopped
	Salt and pepper to taste

1. Heat olive oil in a medium, heavy-bottom skillet over medium high heat. Add onions, reduce heat to medium low, and sauté for 10 to 15 minutes.

2. Deglaze the pan by adding port and red wine; whisk until smooth with an even consistency. Add apples and jam. Cook over low heat until liquid is reduced and mixture is almost dry.

3. Stir in broth and oregano, then add salt and pepper to taste. Cook until mixture has a thick consistency.

4. Serve immediately with any pork dish or store in jars and refrigerate.

Polish Dill Pickles

Recipe donated by Virginia Korpal
MAKES 6 QUARTS

- 36 baby cucumbers, scrubbed clean in cold water
- 2 bunches fresh dill weed
- ¾ cup kosher salt
- 6 garlic cloves, freshly chopped
- ½ cup vinegar
- Cold water

The key to this recipe is finding firm, baby cucumbers. Find them at farmers' markets or farm stands along country roads. The best baby cucumbers are usually available in early August. Select cucumbers that are approximately three inches long, not bruised or cut, with a pleasing, green color. According to European folklore, hanging a dill pickle on the Christmas tree brings good luck throughout the coming year. Today, it is more appropriate to use a glass or ceramic pickle ornament.

1. Tightly pack as many cucumbers as possible in a single layer in a clean, large ceramic crock, approximately 24 inches high. Top with a few sprigs of fresh dill, a sprinkle of kosher salt, and approximately 1 teaspoon chopped garlic. Repeat this process in layers until all cucumbers are used. Sprinkle any remaining dill, salt, or garlic on top.

2. Top cucumbers with vinegar and enough cold water to cover. All cucumbers should be completely submerged. Invert a plate over the cucumbers and top with a clean rock or weight heavy enough to weigh down the plate. Cover crock with a large dishcloth, and tie or band the cloth to secure it over the crock. Place in a cool, dark place, such as a basement or root cellar, and let sit for four to five days.

3. After four days, taste-test the pickles. Add additional salt, if needed. Once the pickles reach the desired taste, transfer from crock to sterilized glass jars. Fill each jar with the brine from the crock, making sure each container includes an equal amount of dill and garlic pieces. Cover and refrigerate before slicing and serving.

4. May be refrigerated for up to five months.

Green Tomato Pickles

Recipe donated by Jim Poutre

MAKES 8 PINTS

- 4 pounds green tomatoes, washed, cored, and cut into ¼-inch thick slices
- 4 medium onions, peeled and sliced
- 1 cup chopped, green pepper
- 2 quarts white vinegar
- 5 cups sugar
- ¼ cup mustard seeds
- 1 tablespoon celery seed
- 1 teaspoon turmeric
- 8 pint jars with lids, sterilized

1. Combine tomatoes, onions, and green pepper. Pack into hot pint jars, filling to ½ inch from the top.

2. Bring approximately 2 to 3 quarts of water to a boil in a large stockpot.

3. Combine vinegar, sugar, mustard seeds, celery seed, and turmeric in a large saucepan. Bring to a boil over high heat. Once sauce boils, pour over tomato mixture in jars. Leave a ½ inch gap from the top; cap with lids and tighten.

4. Place jars in stockpot filled with boiling water. Return water to a boil, allowing jars to boil for 15 minutes. Remove jars from water and set aside to cool.

5. Store in a cool, dry place. Refrigerate after opening.

Ice Pickles

Recipe donated by Ruth Austin
~ MAKES APPROXIMATELY 4 QUARTS

    4 quarts cucumbers, washed and sliced
    8 small onions, peeled and sliced
    2 green peppers, seeded and sliced ½ inch thick
    2 red peppers, seeded and sliced ½ inch thick
    ½ cup kosher salt
    5 cups sugar
  1½ teaspoons cinnamon
    ½ teaspoon cloves
    1 teaspoon celery seed
    1 teaspoon mustard seeds
    5 cups vinegar
    1 cup water

1. Combine cucumbers, onions, green peppers, red peppers, and kosher salt in a large stockpot. Cover with ice, filling to the top of the pot. Let stand for 3 hours; drain and add sugar.

2. Combine cinnamon, cloves, celery seed, mustard seeds, vinegar, and water in a medium saucepan. Bring to boil over high heat. Add to pickles and simmer for 10 to 15 minutes. Pack and seal in sterilized jars.

3. Store in a cool, dry place. Refrigerate after opening.

Chopped Chicken Livers

Recipe donated by Stella Templin
~ SERVES 6 TO 8

- 2 tablespoons chicken fat or butter
- 1 large red onion, peeled and sliced
- 1 teaspoon sugar or brown sugar
- 1 pound chicken livers
- 2 tablespoons butter
- 3 eggs, hardboiled, peeled, and chopped
- 1 teaspoon kosher salt
- 1 teaspoon ground pepper

1. Melt 2 tablespoons chicken fat or butter in a large skillet over low heat. Add onions; sprinkle brown sugar over onions and stir. Cook over low heat, stirring regularly, for approximately 30 minutes, or until onions are caramelized.

2. Rinse chicken livers under cold running water, removing the sinew connecting the livers. Pat dry with paper towels and set aside.

3. Add 2 tablespoons butter to onions and increase heat to medium. Once butter is melted, add chicken livers; stir and brown all sides, cooking for approximately 5 minutes. Reduce heat to low, cover, and cook for an additional 5 minutes. Remove from heat and set aside.

4. Combine chicken livers, onions, and chopped eggs in a medium-sized bowl. Add kosher salt and pepper to taste. Mash livers, onions, and eggs with a potato masher, a hand mixer on low speed, or a food processor on lowest speed until texture is smooth. Let mixture cool for 1 hour, cover, then refrigerate overnight.

5. Serve in a sandwich with raw onions, crisp bacon, and Russian dressing or with a fresh slice of tomato and lettuce, or serve as an appetizer spread on dark rye or pumpernickel points.

Liver Paté

Recipe donated by Riva Arrutsky
~→ SERVES 12

- 2 pounds chicken or veal liver
- 6 tablespoons butter
- 4 large onions, peeled and sliced
- ½ teaspoon salt
- ½ teaspoon pepper
- ¼ teaspoon nutmeg
- ½ cup crushed pistachio nuts (optional)
- 4 slices thin prosciutto (optional)

  Pumpernickel points, French bread, or crackers
  Cornichons for garnish
  Hot mustard for garnish

1. Rinse chicken livers under cold running water, removing the sinew that connects the livers.

2. Bring 4 cups water to a boil in a medium saucepan over high heat. Add liver and return to a boil. Reduce heat to low and simmer for 10 minutes, or until liver is cooked through; drain, rinse, and set aside to cool.

3. Melt butter in a medium-sized skillet over medium high heat. Add onions, reduce heat to low, and sauté until caramelized.

4. Combine liver and onions using a blender, food processor, or a hand mixer in a medium-sized mixing bowl. Add salt, pepper, and nutmeg; mix until liver has a smooth and creamy consistency.

5. Pour mixture into a greased 9-inch loaf pan. You may want to coat the pan with chopped pistachio nuts or sliced prosciutto, allowing you to tap the paté out of the pan more easily.

6. Cover and refrigerate for at least 2 hours. Tap out onto a serving plate and serve with pumpernickel points, French bread, or crackers. Garnish with cornichons and hot mustard.

Chicken Livers and Peppers

Recipe donated by Nona Dreyer

SERVES 8

2 pounds chicken livers

1 cup milk

4 peppers, all colors, seeded and stemmed

2 tablespoons olive oil

3 ribs celery, diced

3 large onions, diced

1 cup red wine vinegar

5 tablespoons sugar

Salt and freshly ground pepper to taste

This is an old, Italian family recipe from my dearest friend's mother-in-law, Mrs. Fierro. When she served these delicious chicken livers and peppers as part of her antipasto, they were devoured within minutes. Even those who don't favor chicken liver will love this easy and unusual preparation that can be made a day in advance.

1. Soak chicken livers in milk in a medium-sized bowl for at least two hours. Rinse with cold running water and cut the sinew with cooking scissors.

2. Cut peppers lengthwise into one-inch strips. Dry with paper towels.

3. Heat olive oil in a large skillet over medium heat. Add peppers, celery, and onions. Cook, covered, for 30 minutes, stirring frequently, until soft.

4. Add chicken livers and cook over low heat for 20 minutes. Pour in red wine vinegar slowly, add sugar, and cook for an additional 10 to 15 minutes, stirring occasionally. Add salt and pepper to taste.

5. Remove from heat and pour into a large mixing bowl; allow to cool. Cover and refrigerate for at least 2 hours.

6. Remove from refrigerator 1 hour before serving.

Apple Spinach Salad

Recipe donated by Inna Spitserev

SERVES 4 TO 6

- 3 apples, cored and sliced
- 3 scallions, chopped
- 3 stalks celery, chopped
- 2 tablespoons lemon juice
- ¼ cup mayonnaise
- ¼ cup sesame paste
- 2 tablespoons honey
- 4 cups fresh spinach leaves, cleaned and torn into bite-sized pieces
- ¼ cup toasted sesame seeds

1. Toss apples, scallions, and celery together in a medium-sized bowl. Add lemon juice and set aside.

2. Combine mayonnaise, sesame paste, and honey in a blender or food processor; blend until thick but smooth. Toss dressing with apples, scallions, and celery. Cover and refrigerate for approximately one hour.

3. To serve, toss spinach with apple mixture in a large salad bowl and sprinkle with sesame seeds.

Orange Salad with Pecan Dressing

Recipe donated by Leo Romero

SERVES 6

    4 oranges, peeled
    1 head Boston lettuce
    2 tablespoons mayonnaise
    2 tablespoons sour cream
    1 tablespoon lime juice
    ½ teaspoon sugar
    ½ teaspoon salt
    ⅛ teaspoon cinnamon
    ⅛ teaspoon black pepper
    ¼ cup chopped pecans

1. Pare and slice oranges and cut sections into quarters. Place in a medium-sized salad bowl.

2. Clean and dry lettuce and tear into bite-sized pieces. Add lettuce leaves to oranges and toss.

3. Combine mayonnaise, sour cream, lime juice, sugar, salt, cinnamon, and pepper in a small mixing bowl; mix well. Stir in chopped pecans.

4. Toss pecan dressing with oranges and lettuce. Serve immediately on chilled salad plates.

Fried Zucchini Blossoms

Recipe donated by Giovanna Covalucci

SERVES 4

This recipe is an old, Italian delicacy. Zucchini blossoms should be very fresh, not wilted. Cut blossoms from their bases and slice in half lengthwise. Remove pistil from the inside of each blossom. Wash quickly under cold running water and dry immediately with paper towels.

- 1 cup water
- 2 large eggs, lightly beaten
- 1 cup flour, sifted
  Salt to taste
- 1/4 cup vegetable oil
- 12 fresh zucchini blossoms, bases trimmed, pistils removed, and halved lengthwise

Dipping Sauce:
- 1/2 cup extra virgin olive oil
- 1 1/2 tablespoons lemon juice or juice of one lemon
- 8 sprigs Italian parsley, chopped extra fine
  Salt and fresh ground black pepper to taste

1. Combine water with beaten eggs in a medium-sized mixing bowl. Gradually add sifted flour, whisking well to avoid any lumps. Season lightly with salt and set aside.

2. Make the dipping sauce in a small bowl by combining olive oil, lemon juice, Italian parsley, and salt and pepper to taste. Mix well and set aside.

3. Place approximately two inches vegetable oil in a large, heavy skillet. Place over medium high heat. When oil is hot, dip a few zucchini blossoms in batter, then carefully place blossoms into pan to fry. When lightly golden on one side, carefully flip over and cook the other side, for approximately 1 minute in total. Remove with slotted spoon and transfer to paper towels to drain. Repeat with remaining zucchini blossoms.

4. Sprinkle drained zucchini blossoms lightly with salt and serve immediately with the dipping sauce.

Vegetable Pancakes with Sour Cream Dill Sauce

Recipe donated by Inna Spitserev

∽ SERVES 4 TO 6

Sauce:

 1 cup sour cream
 2 tablespoons fresh dill, finely chopped
    Salt and pepper to taste

 ¼ pound fresh mushrooms
 ½ cup vegetable oil
 1 medium yellow onion, peeled and finely chopped
 ¼ cup finely chopped celery
 1 cup grated carrots
 1 cup cooked green peas
 2 eggs
 2 tablespoons matzoh meal
 1 tablespoon fresh dill, chopped
    Salt and pepper to taste

1. Make the sauce in a small bowl by mixing sour cream, dill, and salt and pepper to taste. Cover and refrigerate.

2. Clean mushrooms, separate caps from stems, and slice thinly. Place in a small bowl and set aside.

3. Heat ¼ cup vegetable oil in a large skillet over medium heat. Add onions and sauté for 5 minutes. Add mushrooms and celery and sauté for another 5 minutes, or until tender. Remove from heat and set aside to cool.

4. Combine onion sauté, grated carrots, cooked peas, eggs, matzo meal, and dill in a large mixing bowl; mix well. If batter seems watery, add a bit more matzoh meal. Season with salt and pepper to taste.

5. Heat remaining ¼ cup vegetable oil in large skillet over medium heat. Lower heat to medium and slowly ladle approximately ¼ cup vegetable batter, enough to allow 3 pancakes per skillet, onto the fry pan. Keep the pancakes as round as possible. Flip once the pancakes start to brown, and fry until both sides are lightly browned. Remove with slotted spoon and transfer to paper towels to drain.

6. Repeat until all batter is used, adding additional vegetable oil to the skillet as needed.

7. Serve pancakes hot with a tablespoon of sour cream dill sauce on top.

Vegetarian Dolma

Recipe donated by Anna Menshikova
SERVES 8 TO 10

- 1 head green cabbage
- ½ cup vegetable oil
- 2 cups finely chopped onions
- 1 cup finely chopped celery
- 1 cup rice, uncooked
- 1 tablespoon parsley
- ½ cup raisins
- ½ teaspoon cinnamon
- ⅛ teaspoon red pepper
- ½ teaspoon salt
- ½ teaspoon black pepper

1. Remove core of cabbage. Place cabbage, core side down, in a medium stockpot with ½ cup water. Cover and cook over medium heat until cabbage leaves are soft. Drain water and set aside to cool.

2. Heat oil in a medium saucepan over medium heat. Add onions and celery and cook for approximately 5 minutes. Reduce heat to low. Add rice, parsley, raisins, cinnamon, red pepper, salt, and black pepper; mix until all ingredients are combined. Remove from heat and set aside to cool.

3. Preheat oven to 325 degrees.

4. Pull leaves off cooled cabbage and place each leaf bowl-side up to fill. Place ¼ cup of filling onto the stem side of the leaf. Fold in sides and roll the cabbage leaf up firmly around the filling. Pack each rolled cabbage leaf tightly into a 9 by 13-inch baking pan. When all filling is used, pour approximately 3 cups of boiling water over the cabbage rolls in the pan, making sure the water level is approximately half way up the dolmas.

5. Bake until the water is absorbed and the rice is done, approximately 1 hour.

6. Remove from oven and cool. Refrigerate for at least 4 hours and serve cool.

Good on Everything Sauce

Recipe donated by Dorsey B. Baron

MAKES 2 CUPS

- ½ teaspoon tomato paste
- ½ teaspoon vinegar
- ⅛ teaspoon pepper
- 3½ teaspoons dry mustard
- 1   cup mayonnaise
- 2   teaspoons Worcestershire sauce
- 2   tablespoons heavy cream
- 2   tablespoons milk
- ⅛   teaspoon salt

1. Combine tomato paste, vinegar, and pepper in a small mixing dish; mix until smooth.

2. Combine tomato paste mixture, dry mustard, mayonnaise, Worcestershire sauce, heavy cream, milk, and salt in a mixing bowl or shaker; mix or shake vigorously until smooth.

3. Serve sauce with eggs, meat, shellfish, or cheese.

Grandma Mackenzie's Mustard Pickles

Recipe donated by Donald W. Mackenzie
MAKES 6 QUARTS

- 4 large cucumbers, quartered lengthwise, then cut into ½-inch pieces
- 1 large cauliflower, separated into small florets
- 1 large white onion, cut into ⅜-inch bite sized pieces
- ½ cup pickling salt or kosher salt
- 3 quarts cold water

- 6 quart jars with covers, sterilized

Dressing:
- 1 cup flour
- 5 cups sugar
- 1 teaspoon celery seed
- 2 tablespoons dry mustard
- 1 tablespoon turmeric
- 5 cups white vinegar

1. Combine half the cucumbers, cauliflower, and onions in a large stockpot. Sprinkle with ¼ cup pickling or kosher salt, then add the remaining vegetables and another ¼ cup salt. Add 3 quarts cold water to cover cucumber mixture, cover the pot, and let sit overnight in a cool, dry place.

2. Bring the cucumber mixture and brine to a simmer over high heat. Reduce heat to medium and simmer until tender but not soft, approximately 10 minutes. Drain thoroughly, return mixture to the dry stockpot, and set aside.

3. Combine flour, sugar, celery seed, dry mustard, and turmeric in another large stockpot. Gradually add vinegar to the flour mixture over medium heat, stirring constantly to make a smooth paste. Cook over low heat for approximately 5 minutes, stirring constantly.

4. Add the mustard sauce to the drained vegetables and simmer for 5 to 7 minutes. Remove from heat.

This recipe comes from my grandmother who was born in Prince Edward Island, Canada. These are very tasty and were always a favorite. Be careful not to heat the mustard dressing too long. It should be very light. If overcooked, sauce will become too thick.

5. Fill pint-sized jars with hot mustard pickles. Seal jars while hot.

6. Cool sealed jars with pickles to room temperature. Store in a cool, dry place, but refrigerate once opened.

Kiwi Mint Dressing

Recipe donated by Ray Gardiner
~&> MAKES 4 CUPS

     8 kiwi, peeled and sliced
     3 teaspoons whole grain mustard
     4 tablespoons honey
    ½ bunch fresh mint leaves
     1 cup cider vinegar
  1½ cups extra virgin olive oil
  1½ cups vegetable oil
        Salt and pepper to taste

1. Puree kiwi, mustard, honey, mint leaves, and cider vinegar in a blender or food processor. Transfer to a medium-sized mixing bowl.

2. Slowly drizzle in olive oil and vegetable oil; stir well. Season with salt and pepper to taste.

Betty's French Dressing

Recipe donated by Dorsey B. Baron

~ MAKES 2 CUPS

- 1 teaspoon salt
- 2 teaspoons sugar
- 1 teaspoon dry mustard
- ⅛ teaspoon paprika
- 2 teaspoons tarragon vinegar
- ¼ cup red wine vinegar
- ¾ cup extra virgin olive oil

This recipe has been in my family for as long as I can remember. The trick is to get the perfect balance between the sweet and sour tastes. Adjust the amount of sugar and tarragon vinegar to suit your individual taste.

1. Combine salt, sugar, dry mustard, paprika, and tarragon vinegar in a mixing bowl or shaker; mix or shake well. Taste to ensure a good balance of sweet and sour. Add red wine vinegar and olive oil.

2. Mix well before serving with salad or with lettuce leaves topped with grapefruit sections.

Red Horseradish

Recipe donated by Virginia Korpal

MAKES APPROXIMATELY 4 CUPS

1 large horseradish root, peeled
1 large beet, peeled
¾ cup vinegar
4 teaspoons salt
½ cup sugar

If you like horseradish, this is an unbelievable treat, both in taste and color. When peeling and grating the horseradish, be sure you have plenty of windows open because the smell and fumes get intense. You may also want to wear rubber gloves when shredding the beet, and keep plenty of paper towels on hand to wipe up the juices that stain easily.

1. Finely grate horseradish root over a large mixing bowl. Carefully grate beet over horseradish. (You may use a food processor, but the consistency will not be as fine.)

2. Combine vinegar, salt, and sugar in a small mixing bowl; mix well. Pour over horseradish and beets, toss well. Cover and let sit for approximately 1 hour.

3. Taste and add additional vinegar, salt, or sugar to taste.

4. Store in individual jars with some of the juices and refrigerate.

Crab Stuffed Cherry Tomatoes

Recipe donated by Beatrice Griggs
MAKES 20 APPETIZERS

- ½ pound fresh crabmeat
- ½ tablespoon Worcestershire sauce
- ½ tablespoon lemon juice
- 2 8-ounce bricks cream cheese, softened
- 20 cherry tomatoes

1. Combine crabmeat, Worcestershire sauce, lemon juice, and cream cheese in a medium mixing bowl; mix well.

2. Hollow out each tomato from the stem side with a potato peeler, removing stems and seeds.

3. Carefully stuff each tomato with the crab mixture, filling with enough stuffing to reach the top. Cover and refrigerate for at least 4 hours.

Potato Knishes

Recipe donated by Mildred Shorr

~ SERVES 24

  2 tablespoons chicken fat
  1 cup scallions, chopped
  2 cups mashed potatoes
  2 tablespoons sour cream
  ½ teaspoon salt
  ½ teaspoon pepper

Dough:
  2 cups flour
  1 teaspoon baking powder
  ½ teaspoon salt
  2 tablespoons vegetable oil
  2 eggs, lightly beaten
  4 tablespoons water

1. Heat chicken fat in a large skillet over medium heat. Add scallions and sauté until soft. Add mashed potatoes, sour cream, salt, and pepper. Stir until thoroughly heated. Remove from heat and set aside to cool.

2. Combine the flour, baking powder, and salt in a large mixing bowl. Create a small well in the middle of the flour and add the vegetable oil, eggs, and 2 tablespoons water. Mix together. If dough seems too dry, add up to 2 tablespoons of additional water.

3. Form dough into a ball. Place on a lightly floured work surface and knead until smooth. Place dough in an oiled bowl, cover, and refrigerate for 1 hour.

4. Preheat oven to 350 degrees.

5. Divide dough evenly into three sections on a floured work surface. Roll each section to approximately 10 inches long.

Mildred Shorr and Leo Romero of Casa Romero, located in Boston's Back Bay, share stories about their love of cooking.

You can add just about any filling to knishes. Ground beef with onions is another popular favorite. Just substitute your choice of filling for the mashed potatoes and make the knishes as directed.

6. Divide the filling into thirds and spread along the bottom of each dough section, about one inch from the bottom of the strip. Roll up and secure the top layer with a toothpick. Pinch the edges of the rolls tightly to close.

7. Place rolls on an ungreased baking sheet and bake for approximately 40 minutes, or until lightly browned.

8. Remove from oven and allow to cool a few minutes. Slice and serve warm.

Traditional Irish Boxty Appetizer

Recipe donated by Ray Gardiner

SERVES 10

- 1½ pounds potatoes
- 1 white onion
- 3 cups whole milk
- 4 large eggs
- 4 tablespoons butter, melted
- 1 teaspoon tarragon
- 1 teaspoon salt
- 1 teaspoon black pepper
- 3 cups flour
- 1½ tablespoons lemon juice
- 1 teaspoon dill
- 1 tablespoon parsley flakes
- 2 tablespoons plus ¼ cup vegetable oil for frying

Cheddar Dipping Sauce:
- ½ pound butter
- ½ white onion, finely chopped
- ½ carrot, finely shredded
- 1 celery rib, finely diced
- 1 cup flour
- 1 bay leaf
- 1 quart whole milk
- ¾ pound cheddar cheese, grated
- ½ teaspoon salt
- 1 teaspoon pepper

1. Peel and shred potatoes and onion. Squeeze potatoes and onion with a cloth towel or paper towels to soak up excess water and set aside.

2. Mix together milk, eggs, melted butter, tarragon, salt, and pepper in a large bowl. Add potatoes and onion. Add the flour; mix until thick and smooth. Stir in lemon juice, dill, and parsley flakes.

3. In a 10-inch sauté pan, heat two tablespoons oil over medium heat. Pour one cup of batter into pan and cook for approximately 4 to 5 minutes on each side.

4. Remove boxty and cut each pancake into 10 triangular-shaped pieces.

5. Place boxty triangles into a flash fryer and fry until golden brown and crisp. Or, heat ¼ cup vegetable oil in a separate, large, deep skillet over medium heat, add boxty triangles, and fry each side until golden brown and crisp. Remove triangles with slotted spoon and set on paper towels to dry.

6. Make the cheddar dipping sauce by melting the butter over medium heat in a large stockpot. Add the onion, carrot, and celery; sauté until soft. Slowly stir in flour and add bay leaf. Reduce heat and cook for 5 minutes.

7. Increase the heat to medium and slowly add milk, stirring constantly. Remove from heat, then stir in cheddar cheese and salt and pepper.

8. Serve boxty with cheese sauce on the side for dipping.

Mimosa Eggs

Recipe donated by Esme Rajapakse

SERVES 4

- 4 eggs, hardboiled
- ½ cup fresh peas, blanched
- ½ cup baby prawns, cooked and shelled
- 2–3 tablespoons mayonnaise
- ¼ teaspoon tarragon
- Salt and pepper to taste
- Lettuce leaves for garnish
- 1 cucumber, peeled and sliced
- 1 lemon, sliced

1. Cut cooled hardboiled eggs in half and remove yolks. Set whites and yolks aside.

2. Combine peas, baby prawns, mayonnaise, tarragon, and salt and pepper to taste in a small mixing bowl; mix well. Fill each egg white half generously with the prawn mixture.

3. Rub the yolks through a coarse sieve over the tops of the stuffed egg whites so they look like mimosa balls.

4. Serve eggs on top of lettuce leaves and garnish with cucumber slices, additional peas, and lemon slices.

Stuffed Avocado

Recipe donated by Maya Ylyashkevich
SERVES 4

    2 ripe avocados
    1 small white onion, finely chopped
    2 eggs, hardboiled, finely chopped
    2 cloves garlic, finely chopped
  ½ teaspoon lemon juice
    2 teaspoons chopped cilantro
    2 tablespoons mayonnaise

1. Wash outsides of avocados. Cut each into two even halves and remove pits. Scoop meat out, mash, and set aside in a medium-sized mixing bowl. Save avocado shells.

2. Add onion, hardboiled eggs, garlic, lemon juice, cilantro, and mayonnaise to the avocado meat; mix well.

3. Spoon the filling into avocado shells and serve.

Red Caviar

Recipe donated by Sofia Simkina
SERVES 8

1	herring fillet
2	medium carrots, peeled and sliced
1	8-ounce brick cream cheese, softened
1	tablespoon sour cream
¼	pound butter, softened

1. Combine herring, carrots, cream cheese, sour cream, and butter in a blender or food processor. Pulse until mixture is smooth.

2. Pour mixture into a serving bowl and serve with crackers.

Soups & Stews

Homemade Chicken Broth

Recipe donated by Leo Romero
MAKES APPROXIMATELY 7 CUPS

4–5   pound stewing chicken, cut up
   2   medium tomatoes, cut in quarters
   1   rib celery with leaves, chopped
   1   carrot, peeled and diced
   1   onion, peeled and cut into quarters
   3   cloves garlic, chopped
   2   teaspoons salt
   ½   teaspoon dried sage
   ½   teaspoon dried thyme
   ½   teaspoon black pepper

1. Remove any excess fat from the chicken. Place the chicken, neck, and giblets in a large stockpot or 4-quart Dutch oven. Add just enough cold water to cover. Add tomatoes, celery, carrot, onion, garlic, salt, sage, thyme, and pepper. Heat to a boil over high heat.

2. Reduce heat to low, cover, and simmer for 45 minutes or until chicken is tender. Remove from heat and allow to cool. Refrigerate chicken in broth for approximately 2 hours.

3. Remove chicken meat from bones and skin. Skim fat from broth and strain.

4. Place chicken meat and broth in separate containers. Use immediately or refrigerate for up to 24 hours. Broth may also be frozen. Chicken may be used in any soup or recipe calling for cooked chicken.

Homemade Beef Broth

Recipe donated by Leo Romero
MAKES APPROXIMATELY 5 CUPS

- 4 cloves
- 1 onion, peeled and quartered
- 2 pounds beef, chuck, tip, or round
- 2 ribs celery with leaves, chopped
- 2 cloves garlic, minced
- 1 green pepper, seeded and chopped
- 1 bay leaf
- 1 tablespoon oregano
- 1 teaspoon salt
- ½ teaspoon black pepper

1. Insert 1 clove into each onion quarter. Combine beef, onion, celery, garlic, green pepper, bay leaf, oregano, salt, and pepper in a large stockpot or 4-quart Dutch oven. Add just enough cold water to cover. Bring to a boil over high heat.

2. Reduce heat to low and simmer for 2½ to 3 hours or until beef is tender.

3. Remove beef from broth. Skim fat from broth and strain.

4. Place beef and broth in separate containers. Use immediately or refrigerate for up to 24 hours. Broth may also be frozen. Beef may be shredded while warm with two forks for use in soups or recipes calling for cooked beef.

Kluski Noodles

Recipe donated by Louise Kinoske

❧ SERVES 6

These easy-to-make noodles go well with just about any soup. Add to any chicken, duck, or beef soup. They also taste good tossed with melted butter.

- 2 eggs, lightly beaten
- ½ teaspoon salt
- 2¼ cups flour, sifted
- 3 tablespoons lukewarm water

1. Combine beaten eggs in a medium mixing bowl with salt, then add flour a little bit at a time; mix well. Place dough on a flat work surface.

2. Add lukewarm water to dough and work until it becomes elastic and little bubbles appear. Add additional flour if needed. Divide dough into two equal halves.

3. Roll out each section very thinly on a floured surface. Sprinkle a little flour on top of each one, let dough stand a few minutes, then roll up each section. Cut each roll into thin strips about ⅓ inch wide with a paring knife.

4. Fill a medium stockpot ¾ full with water. Add ½ teaspoon salt and bring to a boil over high heat. Add kluski noodles and boil rapidly for 5 to 10 minutes. Drain and serve immediately.

Marrow Dumplings

Recipe donated by Greg Oleszek

SERVES 4

¼ pound beef marrow
2 eggs, separated
   Salt and pepper to taste
2 tablespoons cracker meal or dry breadcrumbs
1 tablespoon fresh dill, chopped
¼ cup flour for rolling

1. Run the beef marrow through a meat grinder. Combine marrow with egg yolks and salt and pepper in a medium mixing bowl; mix well using your hands. Add cracker meal or breadcrumbs, dill, and mix. Set aside.

2. Beat egg whites until stiff in a small mixing bowl. Fold egg whites into beef marrow mixture. Lightly knead mixture.

3. Hand-form mixture into balls approximately 1 inch in diameter.

4. Lightly roll each ball in flour and gently drop into any simmering beef- or vegetable-base soup.

5. Let marrow balls simmer with soup for at least 30 minutes.

Armenian Yogurt Soup

Recipe donated by Inna Spitserev

<small>SERVES 4 TO 6</small>

- 1 tablespoon butter
- 1 onion, peeled and chopped
- 4 cups chicken or vegetable stock, or water
- ¼ cup barley
- 1 egg
- 2 cups plain yogurt
- ¼ cup fresh chopped parsley
- ½ teaspoon dried mint
- Salt and ground white pepper to taste

1. Melt butter in a medium stockpot over medium heat. Add onion and sauté until soft.

2. Add chicken stock, vegetable stock, or water and barley, then simmer over medium low heat until tender, approximately 30 to 45 minutes.

3. Beat egg in a small mixing bowl. Add yogurt and mix until smooth and creamy. Slowly whisk into the soup.

4. Reduce heat to low and cook for 5 minutes, stirring occasionally. Do not let soup come to a boil.

5. Stir in parsley, mint, and salt and white pepper to taste. Serve hot and garnish with fresh parsley.

Macu

Recipe donated by James Accursio
SERVES 4 TO 6

This recipe has been passed down through my family for a few generations. It is a hearty and delicious Sicilian peasant stew. It was created as a highly nutritious dish when meat and/or money were in short supply.

- 3 tablespoons virgin olive oil
- 2 white or yellow onions, peeled and chopped
- 3 carrots, peeled and diced into 1 inch pieces
- 2 pounds fresh fava beans, or 2 14-ounce cans, drained
- 1 bunch fresh escarole, chopped
- 2 quarts chicken stock or water
  Salt and pepper to taste
- 1¼ pounds mixed pasta, (bowtie, small shells, or spaghetti broken into 1 inch pieces)

1. Heat olive oil in a medium stockpot over medium heat. Add onions and carrots and sauté for 3 to 4 minutes.

2. In a small bowl, crush ½ pound of the fava beans with a heavy fork. Add to stockpot.

3. Add remaining whole fava beans, escarole, chicken stock, and salt and pepper to taste. Bring to a boil.

4. Add pasta and enough water to cook pasta, if needed, but not enough to make it soupy.

5. When pasta is al dente, ladle into individual serving bowls and serve.

Thick Tuscan Soup

Recipe donated by Marisa Oliveri

❧ SERVES 4

- 1 cup red or roman beans, cooked
- 1 onion, peeled and cut in quarters
- 1 rib celery, cut into 2-inch sections
- ½ teaspoon fresh or dry basil
- ½ cup peeled tomatoes
- ¼ cup olive oil
- 4 cups water
- 1 cup shredded cabbage
- ¼ cup cornmeal
- Salt and pepper to taste
- Fresh basil and ground pepper for garnish

1. Combine red beans, onion, celery, basil, tomatoes, olive oil, and water in a blender or food processor. Pulse to a coarse texture.

2. Pour mixture into a large saucepan and bring to a boil over high heat. Reduce heat to low, cover, and let simmer for 15 minutes.

3. Stir in shredded cabbage and cornmeal. Allow to simmer for an additional 15 minutes, stirring regularly.

4. Ladle into individual bowls and serve with a garnish of fresh basil, salt, and ground pepper.

Avocado Soup

Recipe donated by Leo Romero

SERVES 6

3 cups chicken broth

1 cup half and half

2 large ripe avocados, peeled and sliced

1 clove garlic, minced

1 tablespoon chopped onion

¾ teaspoon salt

¼ teaspoon fresh cilantro

⅛ teaspoon black pepper

¼ cup sour cream (optional)

1 teaspoon paprika (optional)

1. Combine 1½ cups chicken broth, half and half, sliced avocados, garlic, onion, salt, cilantro, and pepper in a blender or combine in a medium mixing bowl with a hand mixer. Blend until smooth and creamy.

2. Stir remaining chicken broth into avocado mixture. Cover and refrigerate for at least 2 hours.

3. Serve chilled. Ladle into individual bowls and top each with a teaspoon of sour cream and a dash of paprika, if desired.

Baked Potato and Leek Soup

Recipe donated by Ray Gardiner

SERVES 6

    6   potatoes, baked in advance
    2   tablespoons olive oil
    1   white onion, peeled and finely chopped
    1   stalk celery, finely chopped
    1   clove garlic, finely chopped
    1   bunch leeks, cleaned, white ends chopped and greens discarded
    3   bay leaves
 1½   quarts water
    2   cups milk
        Salt and pepper to taste
   ½   cup shredded mix of white and orange cheddar cheese
   ⅛   cup fresh chopped parsley

1. Scoop the flesh out of the potato skins. Set the potato flesh aside and discard the skins.

2. Heat olive oil in a large stockpot over medium high heat. Add onion, celery, garlic, and leeks. Sauté until soft. Add bay leaves, potato flesh, water, milk, and salt and pepper to taste; stir well.

3. Bring to a boil. Reduce heat and simmer for 45 minutes. Puree soup to a smooth consistency using a hand mixer or potato masher.

4. Ladle soup into individual bowls and sprinkle each with cheese and fresh parsley.

Garlic Soup

Recipe donated by Leo Romero
~ SERVES 8

- 2 tablespoons vegetable oil
- 3 cloves garlic, crushed
- 2 slices white bread, cut into 1-inch pieces
- 4 cups chicken broth
- ½ teaspoon salt
- ¼ teaspoon black pepper
- 1 egg, slightly beaten
- ¼ cup fresh chopped parsley (optional)

1. Heat oil in a large saucepan over medium high heat. Add garlic and sauté until brown. Add the bread pieces, stir, and cook until the bread is browned on all sides.

2. Stir in chicken broth, salt, and pepper. Heat to a boil. Reduce heat, cover, and simmer for 20 minutes.

3. Place 2 cups of the hot soup in a small saucepan. Gradually whisk in beaten egg over medium high heat; mix well, then return to soup. Bring soup to a boil again and stir; boil for one minute.

4. Serve hot in individual bowls. Top with fresh parsley, if desired.

Fajitas & 'Ritas Texas Meat Chili

Recipe donated by Brad Fredericks

SERVES 6 TO 8

¾ cup water

1 pound ground beef

1 onion, peeled and chopped

1 green bell pepper, seeded and chopped

½ teaspoon garlic powder

1½ teaspoons cumin

1½ teaspoons black pepper

1 tablespoon salt

½ cup jalapeños, chopped

1¼ cups tomato paste

1¼ cups diced tomatoes in puree

1 15-ounce can kidney beans, drained

Sour cream for garnish (optional)

Shredded cheddar cheese for garnish (optional)

1. Place ¾ cup water in a medium stockpot. Break up ground beef and add to the pot. Cook over high heat until beef is browned. Reduce heat to low.

2. Add onion, green pepper, garlic powder, cumin, black pepper, salt, jalapeños, tomato paste, tomatoes in puree, and kidney beans. Stir, cover, and let simmer for 20 minutes.

3. Serve in large bowls. Top with sour cream and shredded cheese, if desired.

Corn Chowder

Recipe donated by Ruth Austin
SERVES 4

This very old New England recipe has been handed down for many generations. It is easy to make and always tastes best when using fresh corn cut from the cob.

- 6 soda crackers
- 1 cup milk
- 3 slices salt pork, diced
- 1 large onion, peeled and chopped
- 4 large potatoes, peeled and diced
- 2 cups water
- 2 cups fresh cut corn kernels
- 1 teaspoon salt
- ¼ teaspoon paprika

1. Combine soda crackers and milk in a small bowl. Set aside and let soak.

2. Heat salt pork in a medium stockpot over medium heat. Add onion and sauté until soft. Add potatoes and water. Cook until potatoes are soft, approximately 20 minutes.

3. Stir in soda crackers and milk. Add corn, salt, and paprika and simmer for approximately 10 minutes until corn is cooked. Ladle into individual bowls and serve.

Lobster Bisque

Recipe donated by Paul Richardson

SERVES 6

2	tablespoons olive oil
3–4	pounds uncooked lobster pieces; crack body, claws, and tail; keep meat in shell
4	carrots, peeled and sliced
4	medium onions, peeled and diced
4	stalks celery, diced
2	cups dry white wine
¼	cup brandy
3	quarts water
4	cloves garlic, minced
3	tablespoons tomato paste
1	teaspoon paprika
1	pinch cayenne
½	teaspoon thyme
½	teaspoon tarragon
3	bay leaves
2	teaspoons cracked black pepper
¼	cup butter, softened
¼	cup flour
3	cups whipping cream
	Salt and white pepper to taste
¼	cup dry sherry (optional)
2–3	drops red food coloring (optional)

1. Heat olive oil in a large saucepan or small stockpot over high heat until it begins to smoke. Reduce heat to medium, add lobster pieces, stir, and cook until shells turn red. Remove lobster pieces and set aside.

2. Separate shells from lobster meat and return shells to pot. Chop meat into bite-sized pieces and set aside. Add carrots, onions, and celery to pot. Stir, cooking until onions are tender. Add white wine and simmer until wine is reduced by half.

3. Add brandy and bring to a simmer. Carefully ignite with a long stick match, keeping clear from the open flame. When flames die down, add water, garlic, tomato paste, paprika, cayenne, thyme, tarragon, bay leaves, and black pepper; stir well and bring to a boil. Reduce heat and simmer for 35 minutes, stirring occasionally.

4. Strain broth through cheesecloth into a separate saucepan.

5. Combine butter and flour in a small bowl. Knead with your fingers until well combined.

6. Bring lobster stock to a boil. Gradually add butter and flour mixture. Whisk briskly until flour is dissolved and broth is creamy.

7. Heat cream in a small saucepan to almost boiling. Slowly pour hot cream into broth and stir. Add lobster meat and salt and white pepper to taste. Cook at a slow simmer for one minute. Add sherry and food coloring, if desired; stir well.

8. Remove from heat. Ladle into individual bowls and serve.

Bean and Basil Soup

Recipe donated by Beulah Providence
SERVES 6

1 potato, peeled and diced

2 carrots, peeled and diced

1 onion, peeled and chopped

1 teaspoon salt

3 quarts water

2 cups fresh green beans or 2 10-ounce packages frozen green beans

1 cup uncooked macaroni

3 cloves garlic, minced

2 tablespoons fresh basil or 2 teaspoons dried basil

4 tablespoons tomato paste

⅓ cup grated Parmesan cheese

1 tablespoon vegetable oil

2 cups white beans, drained

Beulah Providence, executive director of The Caribbean Foundation of Boston, is pictured above with executive chef Bill Coyne of Boston's most historic restaurant, the Union Oyster House. Ms. Providence founded her agency in 1974, the same year Central Boston Elder Services was started. She learned her love of cooking from her grandmother. Born in Dominica, West Indies, Ms. Providence moved to Boston in the 1960s where her first position was teaching cooking classes to young women.

1. Combine potato, carrots, onion, salt, and 3 quarts water in a large stockpot. Boil over medium high heat until almost tender, approximately 10 to 15 minutes. Add green beans and macaroni. Cook until macaroni is tender, approximately 8 to 10 minutes.

2. Combine garlic, basil, tomato paste, and Parmesan cheese in a medium-sized mixing bowl. Mix in vegetable oil. Slowly add approximately 2 cups hot soup broth, beating vigorously. Pour the mixture back into the soup pot and mix well.

3. Add the white beans and heat through. Ladle into individual bowls and serve hot.

Vegetable Beef Soup

Recipe donated by Beulah Providence
SERVES 8

3	pounds beef shank
2¼	cups tomato juice
⅓	cup chopped onion
2	bay leaves
2	teaspoons Worcestershire sauce
4	teaspoons salt
¼	teaspoon chili powder
2	cups chopped tomatoes
1	cup diced carrots
1¼	cups lima beans
1	cup chopped celery
1	cup peeled and diced potatoes

1. Combine meat, tomato juice, onion, bay leaves, Worcestershire sauce, salt, and chili powder in a large stockpot. Bring to a boil over high heat. Reduce heat to low. Cover and simmer over low heat for approximately 2 hours or until beef is tender.

2. Remove the beef shank from the pot. Cut meat from the bones in large cubes. Skim fat from the broth and strain.

3. Return meat and broth to the stockpot. Add tomatoes, carrots, lima beans, celery, and potatoes. Cover and simmer over low heat for an hour. Ladle into large soup bowls and serve.

Dill Pickle Soup

Recipe donated by Laverne Bansmer
MAKES 6 SERVINGS

- 3 potatoes
- 2 tablespoons flour
- 4 large dill pickles, sliced thin
- 2 tablespoons butter
- 4 cups beef broth
- 1 cup brine from dill pickles
- ½ cup sour cream

1. Peel and cube the potatoes and place in a medium saucepan with enough water to cover. Bring to a boil over high heat. When tender, in approximately 20 minutes, remove from heat, drain, and set aside.

2. Place flour in a small bowl. Coat pickle slices evenly on all sides with the flour.

3. Melt butter in a medium-sized stockpot over medium high heat. Add floured pickle slices and sauté until both sides are browned. Stir in the beef broth, pickle brine, and potatoes. Cook for 15 minutes over medium heat, stirring occasionally.

4. When soup is almost ready, scoop one large tablespoon of sour cream into each serving bowl. Ladle soup over sour cream and serve.

Borscht with Beef Ribs

Recipe donated by Inna Spitserev

~ SERVES 8

- 3 pounds stew beef or beef with ribs
- 2 quarts water
- 1 28-ounce can stewed, chopped tomatoes
- 2 14½-ounce cans shredded beets
- 1 medium onion, chopped
- 1 medium head green cabbage, finely shredded
- 1 14½-ounce can tomato sauce
- 6 medium potatoes, peeled and diced
- ½ teaspoon salt
- ½ teaspoon black pepper
- 1½ tablespoons lemon juice
- 3 gingersnaps, crushed
- 4 tablespoons brown sugar
- ½ teaspoon dill seed
- 1 cup sour cream
- 6 sprigs fresh dill

1. Trim excess fat from the beef or ribs with a sharp knife. Place in a large stockpot and add enough water to cover the meat. Bring to a boil over medium high heat. Simmer for 5 minutes, then drain the water. Remove beef and pull meat from bones, returning meat to stockpot and discarding bones.

2. Add 2 quarts water, tomatoes, beets, onion, cabbage, tomato sauce, potatoes, salt, and pepper to the stockpot; stir in lemon juice. Add gingersnaps and brown sugar and stir. Bring to a boil and simmer for 1½ hours, stirring occasionally. Skim any fat from the top of the soup and continue to simmer for another 30 minutes or until beef is soft and tender.

3. Serve Borscht immediately or remove from the heat, allow to cool, and refrigerate overnight to allow flavors to meld fully. The next day, skim any fat from the top of the soup and bring to a boil. To serve, ladle into soup bowls, then top with one tablespoon of sour cream and a sprig of fresh dill.

Vegetarian Borscht

Vegeta is a popular Russian dried spice mix that may be found in most grocery stores in the international food section.

Recipe donated by Sofia Simkina

SERVES 6

- 2 large beets, peeled
- 3 quarts water
- ½ teaspoon sour salt
- 2 carrots, peeled and sliced
- 1 small green cabbage, finely shredded
- 1 medium onion, peeled
- 2 ribs celery, finely chopped
- 2 red bell peppers, seeded and chopped
- 2 tablespoon olive oil
- 2 cloves garlic, crushed
- 1 tablespoon Vegeta Russian seasoning (optional)
- ½ teaspoon ground red pepper
- ½ teaspoon parsley
- Salt to taste
- 1 cup sour cream
- 6 sprigs of fresh dill

1. Combine beets with 3 quarts water in a large stockpot. Bring to a boil over high heat, boiling until beets are tender. Remove beets and set aside to cool; keep the beet water in the stockpot.

2. Add sour salt to the beet water and mix well. Add carrots, cabbage, onion, celery, and red bell peppers; stir and simmer for 20 minutes.

3. While the stock is simmering, grate beets over a bowl and set aside.

4. Add olive oil, garlic, Vegeta seasoning (if using), red pepper, parsley, and table salt to taste; stir and simmer for 1½ hours. Add the grated beets and accumulated beet juices and simmer for another 5 minutes.

5. Serve Borscht immediately or remove from the heat, allow to cool, and refrigerate overnight to allow flavors to meld fully.

6. The next day, bring the soup to a boil. To serve, ladle into soup bowls, then top with one tablespoon of sour cream and a sprig of fresh dill.

Chilled Borscht

Recipe donated by Irina Kogan

SERVES 6

2 large beets, peeled

1 medium onion, peeled

3 quarts water

½ teaspoon sour salt

½ teaspoon ground red pepper

Salt to taste

1 cup sour cream

6 sprigs of fresh dill

Borscht is one of the most popular Russian dishes. A hearty soup with a pleasing deep red color, it was originally made to feed peasants and farmers. Ingredients vary greatly from region to region. There are many interpretations, but the classic recipe is made from beets, cabbage, and potatoes. In northern regions of Russia, Borscht is traditionally served hot with plenty of sausages, smoked ham, or lamb. In St. Petersburg, meat is replaced with fish or herring and marinated vegetables. In southern, warmer regions, Borscht is lighter, sometimes made using red peppers and tomatoes, and may be served cold or hot. Any way you decide to make Borscht, it tastes best when served the next day to allow the flavors to meld fully.

1. Place the beets and onion in a large stockpot with water. Bring to a boil over medium high heat and simmer until beets are tender. Remove beets and set aside to cool, leaving the onion in the beet water.

2. Add sour salt to the stockpot and mix well. Simmer for 20 minutes.

3. While the stock is simmering, grate beets over a small bowl; set aside.

4. Add red pepper and salt to the soup; stir and simmer for 10 minutes. Add the grated beets and accumulated beet juices and simmer for another 5 minutes.

5. Serve Borscht immediately or remove from the heat, allow to cool, and refrigerate overnight to allow flavors to meld fully.

6. The next day serve the soup chilled or reheated. Remove what is left of the onion before serving. Ladle into individual bowls, then top with one tablespoon of sour cream and a sprig of fresh dill.

Lentil Soup

Recipe donated by Giovanna Covalucci
SERVES 6 TO 8

½ pound lentils
1¼ quarts chicken or vegetable broth or water
½ cup barley
1 medium onion, peeled and finely chopped
1 cup finely chopped celery
1 cup finely diced carrots
1 medium potato, peeled and cubed
3 teaspoons chopped fresh parsley or ½ teaspoon dried parsley
2 bay leaves
1 cup tomato sauce
  Salt and pepper to taste

Garnish:
5 teaspoons extra virgin olive oil
½ cup chopped red onion or broccoli florets

1. Combine lentils, broth or water, barley, onion, celery, carrots, potato, parsley, bay leaves, and tomato sauce in a large stockpot. Bring soup to a boil over high heat.

2. Lower heat to medium and simmer for 45 minutes. Stir occasionally, adding more water or broth if needed. Stir well and add salt and pepper to taste.

3. Remove bay leaves before serving. Ladle into large individual soup bowls. Garnish with a drizzle of extra virgin olive oil, freshly chopped red onion, or broccoli florets.

Minestrone with Pesto

Recipe donated by Giovanna Covalucci

SERVES 6 TO 8

⅛ cup olive oil
2 carrots, peeled and diced
1 medium onion, peeled and chopped
2 ribs celery, chopped
2 cloves garlic, chopped
3½ cups chicken broth
1 cup tomato sauce
1½ cups cannelini or white navy beans, cooked in advance
1 medium savoy cabbage, coarsely chopped
1 medium zucchini, cubed
½ teaspoon pepper
⅛ cup chopped, fresh parsley or ¼ cup dried parsley
¾ cup dry tubetti pasta

Garnish options:
Pesto sauce
Extra virgin olive oil
Fresh grated asiago or romano cheese
Crushed red pepper flakes

Try this quick fresh pesto recipe:

1 cup fresh basil
¼ cup fresh parsley
1 clove garlic, chopped
¼ teaspoon salt
⅓ cup olive oil

1. Combine basil, parsley, garlic, and salt in a food processor; process until smooth.
2. Slowly add olive oil, a little bit at a time, until well mixed.

1. Heat olive oil in a large stockpot over medium high heat. Add carrots, onion, celery, and garlic. Sauté for 8 to 10 minutes or until soft.

2. Add chicken broth, tomato sauce, beans, savoy cabbage, zucchini, pepper, and parsley. Bring to a boil over medium heat. Reduce heat to low and simmer for 45 minutes, stirring occasionally.

3. Add pasta and cook for an additional 15 minutes.

4. Ladle into large soup bowls. Garnish with pesto, drizzle with extra virgin olive oil, and top with grated asiago or romano cheese or crushed red pepper.

Zucchini Soup

Recipe donated by Inna Spitserev
SERVES 6 TO 8

- 2 cups grated unpeeled zucchini
- 1 medium potato, peeled and grated
- 1 teaspoon butter or vegetable oil
- 1 leek, washed, white section chopped and greens discarded
- 6 scallions, greens and whites, chopped
- 1 white onion, peeled and chopped
- 4 cups chicken or vegetable stock

    Salt and pepper to taste

Garnish options:

    Fresh chopped parsley
    Fresh chopped dill

1. Strain the zucchini and potato to drain off excess liquid.

2. Heat butter or oil in a medium saucepan over medium high heat. Add zucchini, potato, leek, scallions, and onion. Sauté until soft.

3. Bring broth to a boil over high heat in a large stockpot. Add sautéed vegetables, then stir and simmer over low heat for 30 minutes. Add salt and pepper to taste.

4. Ladle into large soup bowls. Garnish with fresh chopped parsley or fresh chopped dill.

Czarnina–Polish Duck Soup

Recipe donated by Louise Kinoske

SERVES 10

1	duck, cut in pieces
1½	pound pork loin back ribs
2	quarts water
2	teaspoons salt
1	stalk celery, chopped
1	parsley sprig
5	whole allspice
2	whole cloves
1	pound dried, pitted prunes
½	cup raisins
1	apple, peeled, cored, and chopped
2	tablespoons flour
1	tablespoon sugar
1	cup whipping cream or sour cream
1	quart duck, goose, or pork blood (with vinegar, available at butcher shops on request)
1	tablespoon lemon juice
1	tablespoon vinegar
	Salt and pepper to taste
1	pound noodles or homemade kluski noodles (see page 70), cooked

1. Combine duck and pork ribs in a large stockpot with enough water to cover. Add salt. Bring to a boil over high heat. Skim off fat.

2. Place celery, parsley, allspice, and cloves in a cheesecloth bag, tie, and add to soup. Cover and cook over low heat for approximately 1½ hours or until meat is tender.

3. Remove spice bag from soup.

4. Remove duck and pork ribs from soup and set aside to cool. Remove bones and cut meat into bite-sized pieces. Return meat to soup.

5. Add prunes, raisins, and apple; stir and simmer for 30 minutes.

6. Combine flour, sugar, and whipping cream or sour cream in a large mixing bowl; mix until smooth. Slowly add duck blood mixture a little at a time until well blended. Add ½ cup of the hot soup stock and beat until smooth.

7. Pour the cream mixture slowly into the soup, stirring constantly. Add lemon juice, vinegar, and salt and pepper to taste. Bring to a boil.

8. Ladle into individual bowls and serve with homemade kluski noodles or other noodles.

Spinach Rhubarb Soup

Recipe donated by Steve Snow

SERVES 4 TO 6

This recipe has been in my family for over 100 years. It originally came from Russia with my grandmother. It's great in the springtime when you can get fresh, young rhubarb. The lemon juice and sugar levels should be adjusted to taste due to variances in the tartness of the rhubarb.

- 1 package fresh spinach, washed and stems removed
- 1½ pounds rhubarb, washed and cubed
- 2 scallions, greens and whites, chopped
- ½ teaspoon salt
- 4–6 tablespoons sugar
- 2 tablespoons lemon juice
- 2 quarts water

Garnish options:
    Chopped scallions
    Chopped hardboiled eggs
    Fresh dill

1. Combine spinach, rhubarb, and scallions in a large stockpot and fill with enough water to cover. Cover pot and bring to a boil over high heat.

2. Add salt, 4 tablespoons sugar, and lemon juice. Simmer, uncovered, for approximately one hour. Taste and add additional lemon juice or sugar, if needed. There should be a balance in taste between sweet and sour.

3. Remove from heat and allow to cool. Cover and refrigerate overnight.

4. Serve chilled with fresh chopped scallions, chopped hardboiled eggs, or a fresh dill sprig on top.

Oxtail Soup

Recipe donated by Paul Richardson
SERVES 6

2	oxtails
1	tablespoon flour
3	tablespoons fat or butter
1	carrot, peeled and diced
1	large onion, peeled and chopped
2	quarts beef stock, vegetable stock, or water
2	stalks celery
1	bay leaf
2	sprigs parsley
2	tablespoons barley
¼	teaspoon salt
¼	teaspoon pepper
¼	teaspoon cayenne pepper
1	teaspoon Worcestershire Sauce
¼	cup sherry or dark red wine

1. Place oxtails in a bowl and lightly flour all sides. Melt fat or butter in a large stockpot over medium heat. Add carrot, onion, and oxtails; cook, stirring, until oxtails are brown on all sides. Add stock or water.

2. Tie celery stalks, bay leaf, and parsley together with a piece of kitchen twine and add to soup. Bring to a boil, stir in barley, and simmer over low heat for approximately 1½ hours. Skim off fat. Add salt, pepper, and cayenne pepper. Simmer for an additional 1½ hours.

3. Skim off fat again. Remove celery, bay leaf, and parsley. Remove oxtails, pull meat off the bones, and return meat to soup. Stir in Worcestershire sauce and sherry or wine.

4. Ladle into soup bowls and serve while hot.

Cauliflower Soup

Recipe donated by Stella Templin
❧ SERVES 6 TO 8

- ½ cup fresh mushrooms, finely sliced
- 2 tablespoons butter
- 1 cauliflower
- 1 teaspoon salt
- 6 cups chicken or vegetable stock
- 1 tablespoon flour
- 3 egg yolks
- ½ cup heavy cream
- Salt and pepper to taste
- Fresh croutons or toast points for garnish

1. Sauté mushrooms with 1 tablespoon butter in a small saucepan until translucent. Remove from heat and set aside.

2. Place cauliflower in a large stockpot, head side up, fill with cold water to cover, and add 1 teaspoon salt. Bring to a boil over high heat. Reduce heat to low and simmer for approximately 30 minutes. Remove cauliflower head and place in a mixing bowl to cool; discard the water used for boiling.

3. Add chicken or vegetable stock to stockpot and bring to a boil over medium high heat. Reduce heat to low and continue to simmer.

4. Combine remaining 1 tablespoon butter and flour in a small bowl to make a paste. Add 3 tablespoons of hot broth; stir until smooth. Slowly stir paste into stock.

5. Remove 10 florets from the head of cauliflower and set aside; mash the rest with a potato masher. Add mashed cauliflower to stock and mix well.

6. Combine egg yolks with heavy cream in a small bowl and beat until smooth. Add a little of this mixture at a time to the stock while constantly stirring to avoid any curdling. Season with salt and pepper to taste. Continue to simmer, stirring regularly. Add sautéed mushrooms and reserved cauliflower florets. Simmer for an additional 10 minutes.

7. Ladle into soup bowls and serve with fresh croutons or toast points.

Split Pea and Ham Soup

Recipe donated by Virginia Korpal

SERVES 8 TO 10

- 1 pound dried green split peas
- 4 cups cold water
- 1 hambone with extra meat
- 1 medium onion, peeled and left whole
- 1 medium onion, peeled and chopped
- 1 clove garlic, finely chopped
  Black pepper to taste
- 2 cups cold water
- 3 carrots, peeled and diced
- 2 potatoes, peeled and diced

1. Wash green split peas and place in large mixing bowl with 4 cups cold water. Cover and let soak overnight.

2. Remove extra meat from a leftover hambone, trim fat, and refrigerate.

3. Place the hambone and whole onion in a large stockpot with enough water to cover. Bring to a boil and simmer for approximately 4 to 5 hours, or until the bone comes clean. Remove from heat and cool for approximately 2 hours. Skim fat from the top and refrigerate overnight.

4. The next day, again skim fat from the top of the broth. Remove hambone and discard. Strain broth and place in a clean stockpot.

5. Drain green split peas and add to stockpot with ham broth. Add chopped onion, garlic, black pepper, and approximately 2 cups cold water. Bring to a boil over medium heat; reduce heat, cover, and simmer for approximately 2 hours, or until peas are tender.

6. Use a potato masher or hand mixer to puree the soup. Add diced carrots, potatoes, and leftover ham pieces and simmer. If soup is too thick, add an additional cup of cold water and stir. Cook until carrots and potatoes are soft, about 30 minutes. Add black pepper to taste and stir.

7. Ladle into large soup bowls and top with croutons or toast points.

Union Oyster House Fish Chowder

Recipe donated by Bill Coyne

SERVES 6

- 1 pound cusk or other firm boneless white fish
- 4 cups fish broth or stock
- ½ pound potatoes, peeled and diced
- 1 ounce salt pork
- 1 celery rib, minced
- 1 small onion, peeled and diced
- 2 tablespoons butter
- ¼ cup flour
- 5 drops Worcestershire sauce
- 5 drops Tabasco sauce
- 1 pint half and half

1. Steam or poach fish in broth or stock in a large, heavy-bottom soup pot. Remove fish, cut into bite-sized pieces, and set aside.

2. Add potatoes to stock, bring to a boil, and simmer for 15 to 18 minutes, or until tender.

3. While potatoes are cooking, place salt pork in a small pan and cook over medium heat until fat melts. Add celery and onion and sauté for a few minutes. Add to stock.

4. Place butter in a small saucepan and melt over low heat. Add flour and stir for a few minutes to make a roux.

5. When potatoes are just about tender, whisk roux into stock. Season with Worcestershire sauce and Tabasco sauce. Add fish pieces and half and half; stir gently until well mixed.

6. Serve hot with oyster crackers.

Union Oyster House Clam Chowder

Recipe donated by Bill Coyne

SERVES 8 TO 10

- 1 pound potatoes, peeled and diced
- 4 cups clam juice
- 2 pounds clams, fresh or frozen, diced
- ¼ cup salt pork, skinned and diced
- 1 small onion, peeled and diced
- ¼ pound butter
- ¼ cup flour
- 1 pint half and half
- 5 drops Worcestershire sauce
- 5 drops Tabasco sauce
  Salt and pepper to taste
  Oyster or pilot crackers for garnish

1. Place potatoes and clam juice in a large soup pot and bring to a boil over high heat. Reduce heat and let simmer until potatoes are tender. Add clams and any juices, and cook for a few minutes until clams are tender. Be sure to not overcook as clams will become tough. Remove from heat and set aside.

2. Place salt pork in a medium saucepan and cook over medium heat until fat melts. Add onion and sauté until translucent. Stir in butter until melted, then slowly add flour and stir until sauce becomes a roux. If mixture is thin, add a little more flour. Cook until slightly colored.

3. Return potatoes and clams to a boil. Whisk roux into stock. Bring to a rolling boil, stirring regularly.

4. Heat half and half to a simmer in a medium saucepan over medium heat. Stir into chowder, then add Worcestershire, Tabasco, and salt and pepper to taste.

5. Serve with oyster or pilot crackers.

Chicken Stew

Recipe donated by Maltsya Batelman
SERVES 6

6 chicken legs
2 tablespoons olive oil
2 large onions, chopped
5 cloves garlic, chopped
3 cups water
½ cup apple juice
4 tablespoons soy sauce
⅛ teaspoon nutmeg
  Salt and pepper to taste
4 tablespoons paprika
4 tablespoons cranberry sauce
2 red bell peppers, seeded and cut in half

1. Remove and discard fat and skin from the chicken legs. Set meat aside.

2. Heat olive oil in a large saucepan over medium high heat. Add onions and garlic; sauté until golden brown.

3. Add water, apple juice, soy sauce, nutmeg, salt and pepper to taste, paprika, and cranberry sauce. Bring to a boil. After 1 minute, add chicken and pepper halves.

4. Cover and simmer over low heat for approximately 2 hours (cook for less time if you like firm meat). Remove chicken from pot and set aside.

5. Remove pepper halves from pot and peel off skins; return red pepper flesh to pot.

6. Puree sauce with a hand mixer or transfer to a blender and puree until smooth. Taste for salt, pepper, and garlic, adding more if needed.

7. Pour sauce over chicken and serve over rice, mashed potatoes, or noodles.

Tripe Stew

Recipe donated by Leo Romero
~ SERVES 8

    2 pounds honeycomb tripe
    4 cloves
    1 onion, peeled and quartered
    3 cups chicken broth
    2 cups water
    ½ cup chopped carrots
    ½ cup chopped celery
    2 cups whole tomatoes, peeled
    3 cloves garlic, finely chopped
    1 teaspoon salt
    ½ teaspoon oregano
    ½ teaspoon sage
    ½ teaspoon pepper
    1 tablespoon olive oil
    ¼ cup chopped scallions, white and green

1. Rinse tripe under cold water. Place tripe in a bowl and add enough cold water to cover. Let stand for 2 hours. Drain and rinse again.

2. Add cold water and let sit for an additional 2 hours. Drain and rinse again. Cut into strips approximately 2 inches by ¼ inch. Set aside.

3. Insert one clove into each onion quarter.

4. Combine tripe, onion, chicken broth, water, carrots, celery, whole tomatoes, garlic, salt, oregano, sage, and pepper in a large saucepan or stockpot. Bring to a boil. Reduce heat, cover, and simmer until tripe is tender, for approximately 4 hours. When tripe is tender, stir in olive oil.

5. Ladle into soup bowls and sprinkle with chopped scallions.

Green Chile Chicken Stew

Recipe donated by Anne Walker
 SERVES 4 TO 6

     1 tablespoon olive oil
     1 large onion, peeled and chopped
     2 cloves garlic, minced
     2 pounds chicken breast, skinned, boned, and cut into 1-inch chunks
  2–3 cups tomatoes, chopped and seeded
     4 cups hominy (or several Yukon Gold potatoes, boiled and
        coarsely chopped)
    12 green Anaheim chile peppers, roasted, peeled, seeded, and chopped
        coarsely (or canned, chopped chili peppers)
  6–8 cups chicken stock
  1½ tablespoons cumin
     2 tablespoons chili powder
     2 teaspoons ground coriander
     2 teaspoons fresh chopped oregano
     2 teaspoons fresh chopped cilantro
        Salt and pepper to taste

Garnish options:
        Fresh chopped cilantro
        Finely chopped onion
        Slices of lime
        Chopped jalapeño peppers
        Fresh chopped oregano
        Heated corn tortillas

1. Heat olive oil in a heavy stockpot over medium heat. Sauté onions and garlic until slightly softened, approximately 5 minutes.

2. Add chicken and cook over low heat until just cooked through. Add tomatoes and cook until they give off their juices.

3. Add hominy or potatoes, chile peppers, chicken stock, cumin, chili powder, coriander, and oregano to the chicken stock. The ingredients should be covered by approximately 1 inch of liquid. Simmer over low heat for approximately one hour.

4. Add chopped fresh cilantro and salt and pepper to taste.

5. Ladle into soup bowls, garnish with choice of toppings, and serve with heated corn tortillas.

Lobster Stew

Recipe donated by Dorsey B. Baron
SERVES 6

2 lobsters
6–8 small red potatoes, washed in cold water
2 tablespoons butter
1 onion, peeled and chopped
2 stalks celery, chopped
2 carrots, peeled and chopped
1 green pepper, seeded and chopped
1 red pepper, seeded and chopped
4 scallions, chopped
1 cup evaporated milk
2 cups whole milk
1 cup dry sherry
½ teaspoon salt
¼ teaspoon pepper

1. Fill a large stockpot or lobster pot approximately ¾ full with water. Bring to a boil over high heat. Add lobsters and cook until they turn bright red, approximately 15 to 20 minutes. Remove lobsters and set aside to cool. Discard water.

2. Boil potatoes in enough water to cover in a medium saucepan until tender, approximately 20 minutes. Remove potatoes and set aside to cool. Reserve potato cooking water.

3. Heat 1 tablespoon butter in a large stockpot over medium heat. Add onion, celery, carrots, green pepper, red pepper, and scallions. Sauté until soft. Add 2 cups potato cooking water.

4. Cut potatoes into quarters and add to stockpot. Stir in evaporated milk, whole milk, and dry sherry. Reduce heat to low.

5. Break apart lobsters over a large bowl. Remove meat and tamale and set aside. Return shells, along with any accumulated lobster juices, to the stew. Cut lobster meat into bite sized chunks.

6. Heat remaining tablespoon butter in a medium skillet over medium heat. Add lobster meat and sauté for five minutes. Add to stew.

7. Add salt and pepper to taste. Cover and simmer over low heat for 1½ hours, stirring regularly.

8. Remove lobster shells from stew, ladle into bowls, and serve while hot.

Spicy Peanut Soup

Recipe donated by Rita O'Hare

SERVES 6

- 2 tablespoons olive oil
- 3 cloves garlic, finely chopped
- 3 medium onions, peeled and chopped
- 2 large red bell peppers, seeded and diced
- 4 cups chicken broth
- 4 cups water
- ½ teaspoon fresh-ground black pepper
- ½ teaspoon ground red pepper
- 3½ cups crushed tomatoes
- ½ cup rice
- 1 cup chunky peanut butter
- 2 cups cubed chicken breast, cooked in advance

1. Heat olive oil over medium heat in a large Dutch oven or stockpot. Add garlic, onions, and red bell peppers; sauté until soft, approximately 10 minutes.

2. Stir in chicken broth, water, black pepper, red pepper, and crushed tomatoes. Simmer for 45 minutes.

3. Add rice. Cover and simmer for an additional 20 minutes.

4. Whisk in peanut butter and stir until thoroughly blended. Add cooked chicken. Simmer for 10 minutes.

5. Ladle into individual bowls and serve.

Chaleh Bibi

Recipe donated by Safta Malka Sedighi

✎ SERVES 8 TO 10

- 1 cup dried kidney beans
- 1 cup dried mung beans
- 1 cup dried lentils
- 1 cup white rice
- 2 small white turnips, peeled and diced in ½-inch pieces
- 1 head garlic, cloves diced
- 2 medium onions, peeled and chopped
- 1 pound stew beef, cut into 1-inch cubes
- 2 pounds soup bones
- ¼ head red cabbage, shredded
- 8–10 eggs, hardboiled and peeled (optional)
  Lemon juice to taste
  Salt and pepper to taste

This dish, translated "aunt" or "grandma" is originally from Shiraz, in southern Iran. This is a thick and heavy Jewish stew with an almost mush consistency. It is usually made in winter, especially for Shabbat, and as the original recipe card notes, it is customarily served with vodka or Pepsi! This tastes best when it's slow-cooked overnight for approximately twelve hours.

1. Pick through kidney beans, mung beans, and lentils to remove any pebbles. Rinse thoroughly, place in a medium bowl, fill with water to cover, and let soak for an hour.

2. Combine white rice, kidney beans, mung beans, lentils, turnips, garlic, onions, beef, soup bones, and red cabbage in a large stockpot. Add water to within two inches of the top of the pot. Cover and bring to a boil over high heat. Reduce heat to low and cook overnight, the longer the better, stirring occasionally. Add water occasionally to maintain soup consistency.

3. Add hardboiled eggs to chaleh bibi one hour before serving, if desired.

4. Before serving, season with lemon juice and salt and pepper to taste.

Lamb Stew

Recipe donated by Evelyn L. Schroeder
~ SERVES 6 TO 8

- 2 pounds lamb, cubed
  Salt and pepper to taste
- 2 tablespoons fat or lard
- 2 medium onions, peeled and chopped
- 2 carrots, peeled and diced
- 2 cups tomatoes, peeled
- 1 cup green peas
- 1 teaspoon salt
- ¾ teaspoon pepper
- 1 cup beef broth
- ¼ cup soy sauce, to taste
- 1 bunch fresh parsley

1. Season lamb with salt and pepper.

2. Melt fat or lard in a large skillet or roaster with a cover over medium high heat. Add lamb and brown on all sides. Add onions and carrots and sauté for 10 minutes.

3. Reduce heat to medium low. Add tomatoes, green peas, salt, pepper, and beef broth. Stir and simmer for at least one hour, or until meat is tender.

4. When meat is almost tender, add soy sauce to taste. Serve hot with sprigs of fresh parsley.

Main Courses

Cauliflower and Noodles

Recipe donated by Josephine Arena
 SERVES 4

- 1 large cauliflower, cleaned and cut into ½ inch cubes
- 2 tablespoons olive oil
- 1 large onion, peeled and chopped
- 2 cloves garlic, finely chopped
- 2 cups chopped fresh tomatoes
- 1 tablespoon fresh basil, finely chopped
- ⅛ teaspoon sugar
    Salt and pepper to taste
- ½ pound medium-width egg noodles

1. Place approximately 5 cups salted water in a large saucepan and bring to a boil over high heat. Add cauliflower pieces, reduce heat to medium, and cook until tender.

2. Heat olive oil in a large skillet over medium heat. Add onion and garlic; sauté until golden brown. Add tomatoes and cook for 12 minutes at a high simmer. Stir in basil and sugar. Add salt and pepper to taste.

3. Bring 8 cups of water to a boil in a large saucepan; add noodles and cook for approximately 8 to 10 minutes, or until tender with some bite.

4. Drain cauliflower well. Place in bowl and mash with a potato masher. Add mashed cauliflower to tomato mixture. Stir well.

5. Drain noodles. Add to cauliflower and tomato mixture and gently stir to coat the noodles. Serve in shallow bowls.

Pasta Fagioli Alla Fresca

Recipe donated by Josephine Arena
SERVES 6

2 pounds fresh shell beans, shelled, rinsed, and drained
3 tablespoons fresh chopped basil
   Salt and fresh ground pepper to taste
2 tablespoons olive oil
1 large onion, finely chopped
2 cloves garlic, finely chopped
4 large tomatoes, peeled and pureed
½ cup tiny pasta shells
¼ cup grated Parmesan cheese

These recipes from the Arena family of Arena Farms in Concord, Massachusetts, have been made for four generations. They were passed down to Josephine "Bobbie" Arena from her mother and grandmother from the hills of northern Sicily near Palermo. Like much of the food made generations ago, these dishes are plain, simple, satisfying, and delicious. That they pick the ingredients fresh from the garden is the most important single factor that makes the Arena family's cooking so delicious.

1. Combine beans with just enough water to cover in a medium flameproof casserole dish. Bring to a boil over high heat. Reduce heat to medium low. Add basil and salt and pepper to taste. Simmer over low heat for ten minutes.

2. Heat olive oil over medium heat in a small skillet. Add onion and sauté for five minutes. Add garlic and sauté until onion is soft, but not brown. Add onion and garlic to the casserole dish with the beans.

3. Stir in tomato puree and simmer for 45 minutes or until the beans are tender.

4. Bring 5 cups of water to a boil in a medium saucepan over high heat. Add pasta shells and simmer for 8 minutes or until tender with some bite. Drain the pasta, reserving ¾ cup pasta water.

5. Add pasta to the bean casserole. Add salt and pepper to taste. Add pasta water to the beans to achieve a loose consistency, but do not let it get soupy.

6. Ladle into shallow bowls. Sprinkle with Parmesan cheese.

Fried Noodles

Recipe donated by Esme Littleton
SERVES 4

½ pound ramen egg noodles or thin spaghetti
1 teaspoon plus 2 tablespoons vegetable oil
¾ cup cooked chicken pieces
½ cup shredded cabbage
½ cup chopped onion
¼ cup bean sprouts
½ cup sliced mushrooms
1½ tablespoons soy sauce
½ cup cooked ham pieces
½ cup shredded lettuce
Salt to taste

1. Cook noodles following instructions on package. Drain and toss with 1 teaspoon of oil; set aside.

2. Heat 2 tablespoons vegetable oil over medium heat in a large, deep skillet. Add chicken and brown on all sides, approximately 8 minutes. Add cabbage, onion, bean sprouts, and mushrooms. Stir well and cook for approximately 4 minutes.

3. Add cooked noodles, soy sauce, and half the ham; toss well, making sure noodles are well-coated. Add salt to taste and toss noodles again.

4. Place noodles on a serving plate and garnish with shredded lettuce and the remaining ham.

Tortellini and Cauliflower Zuppeta

Recipe donated by Janet Vaglica
SERVES 4

- 4 cups plum tomatoes, cored, peeled, crushed, and chunky
- ½ cup olive oil
- 2 cloves garlic, finely chopped
- 4 leaves fresh basil, chopped
- Salt and pepper to taste
- 1 head cauliflower, cored, florets separated
- 1 pound cheese tortellini
- 1 teaspoon salt
- ½ cup Romano cheese
- ½ cup Parmesan cheese

1. Combine tomatoes, olive oil, garlic, basil, and salt and pepper to taste in a large saucepan. Bring to a boil. Reduce heat and let simmer for at least 35 minutes.

2. Combine cauliflower, tortellini, and salt in a large stockpot with enough water to cover. Bring to a boil over high heat. Reduce heat and simmer until cauliflower is tender, approximately 20 minutes. Drain and place tortellini and cauliflower into a large pasta bowl.

3. Top with tomato sauce, sprinkle with Romano and Parmesan cheese, and serve.

Crabmeat Casserole

Recipe donated by Beulah Providence
SERVES 6 TO 8

- 6 tablespoons butter
- 4 tablespoons flour
- 2 cups milk
- ½ cup shredded cheddar cheese
- ½ teaspoon salt
- ¼ teaspoon pepper
- 2 tablespoons dry sherry
- 2 eggs, lightly beaten
- 1 pound fresh, frozen (thawed), or canned crabmeat

Topping:
- 2 tablespoons butter
- 2 tablespoons shredded cheddar cheese
- ½ cup dry breadcrumbs

1. Preheat oven to 350 degrees.

2. Melt 4 tablespoons of butter in a medium saucepan over medium heat. Whisk in flour and milk slowly, stirring constantly, until the mixture is smooth and thick.

3. Add ½ cup shredded cheese and stir until melted. Remove from heat. Add salt, pepper, dry sherry, and eggs; mix well.

4. Spread crabmeat evenly over the bottom of a 2-quart casserole dish or 9-inch pie pan. Pour cheese mixture over crabmeat.

5. Melt 2 tablespoons butter in a medium saucepan over medium heat. Add 2 tablespoons cheese and stir until melted. Stir in breadcrumbs. Consistency should be crumb-like. Sprinkle evenly over the crabmeat mixture.

6. Bake for 25 minutes. Remove from oven and allow to cool for a few minutes. Cut into slices and serve with a green salad, fresh asparagus, or fruit salad.

Hot Chicken Salad

Recipe donated by Norma Von Fricken
SERVES 4 TO 6

- 4 cups cooked chicken pieces
- 2 cups chopped celery
- 2 cups fresh toasted croutons
- 1 cup mayonnaise
- ¼ cup chopped onion
- 1 teaspoon salt
- ⅛ teaspoon pepper
- 1 cup Swiss cheese, shredded or sliced into strips
- ¼ cup almonds, toasted

1. Preheat oven to 350 degrees.

2. In a large mixing bowl, combine chicken pieces, celery, toasted croutons, mayonnaise, onion, salt, pepper, and Swiss cheese; mix well until all ingredients are coated with mayonnaise.

3. Pour chicken mixture into a 2-quart casserole dish. Sprinkle the top with toasted almonds.

4. Cover and bake for 30 to 40 minutes. Serve while hot.

Chicken Crab Divan

Recipe donated by Cynthia E. Blain
SERVES 6 TO 8

    8 tablespoons butter
    4 whole chicken breasts, halved, skinned, and boned
   ½ pound fresh crabmeat
   ¼ cup dry sherry
    2 teaspoons kosher salt
    1 teaspoon fresh ground pepper
   ½ cup fresh mushrooms, quartered
   ¼ cup chopped onion
    2 cloves garlic, minced
    3 tablespoons flour
 1⅓ cups heavy cream
    1 cup milk
   ½ cup fresh chopped parsley
   ⅛ teaspoon cayenne pepper
   ¼ cup freshly grated Parmesan cheese
    2 jars artichoke hearts (15 ounce size), regular or marinated, drained
    1 teaspoon paprika

1. Heat 4 tablespoons butter in a large cast iron skillet or Dutch oven over medium heat. Add chicken and cook approximately 15 minutes or until juices run clear. Add crabmeat and cook for 4 to 5 minutes. Add sherry and sauté for 1 minute, allowing alcohol to evaporate. Season with kosher salt and ground pepper. Remove chicken and crabmeat from pan; set aside and cover to keep warm. Leave the juices in the pan.

2. Add remaining 4 tablespoons butter to juices in pan and sauté mushrooms, onion, and garlic over medium heat. Stir in flour. Gradually add cream and milk, stirring constantly. Add parsley and cayenne pepper. Remove from heat. Stir in Parmesan cheese.

3. Preheat oven to 375 degrees.

4. Arrange artichoke hearts on the bottom of a greased, 9 by 13-inch baking pan. Cover with half the mushroom and onion sauce and layer with chicken and crabmeat. Top with remaining mushroom and onion sauce. Sprinkle with paprika.

5. Bake for 20 minutes, being careful not to let it burn. Serve hot with rice or mashed potatoes.

Mexican Chicken

Recipe donated by Leo Romero
SERVES 6

- ½ cup vegetable oil
- 1 onion, peeled and sliced thick
- 4 tomatoes, chopped
- ½ cup water
- 12 green olives, pitted
- 2 stalks celery, chopped
- 2 tablespoons capers
- 2 cloves garlic, finely chopped
- 2 bay leaves
- 1 tablespoon oregano
- 1 teaspoon salt
- ¼ teaspoon pepper
- 6 chicken breasts, boned
- 1 cup sliced mushrooms

1. Heat vegetable oil in a large skillet over high heat. Add onion and reduce heat to medium; cook until tender.

2. Stir in tomatoes, water, olives, celery, capers, garlic, bay leaves, oregano, salt, and pepper. Bring to a boil; reduce heat to low and let simmer uncovered for 10 minutes.

3. Arrange chicken breasts skin-side up in a single layer in the skillet. Cover and cook for 15 minutes. Add mushrooms, cover, and cook until chicken is cooked through, approximately 5 minutes longer.

4. To serve, pour sauce on top of chicken breasts. Serve while hot.

Southern Egg Dumplings and Chicken

Recipe donated by Ruth Austin
SERVES 4

2	eggs
1¼	cups flour
¼	cup instant nonfat dry milk
½	teaspoon baking powder
8	cups chicken stock or broth
3	cups chicken, cooked and coarsely chopped
	Salt and pepper to taste

1. Beat eggs in a medium mixing bowl. Sift together flour, instant nonfat dry milk, and baking powder. Slowly add to beaten eggs. Stir until thick. Knead and form dough into a ball. Divide ball in half.

2. Bring chicken stock to a boil in a large stockpot over medium high heat.

3. Roll each half of the dough very thin on a well-floured board or a work surface. Cut dough into 1 by 3-inch strips with a sharp knife. Stretch each strip and drop, one at a time, into the boiling chicken broth. Cover and simmer over low heat for approximately 45 minutes.

4. Stir in chicken pieces and continue to simmer until dumplings are tender. Add salt and pepper to taste. Serve hot in individual bowls.

Chicken Supreme

Recipe donated by Pennie Roche

☙ SERVES 8

- ¼ pound butter
- ½ cup flour
- ½ teaspoon salt
- ½ teaspoon pepper
- 2 pounds boneless chicken, cut into large pieces
- 1 pound fresh mushrooms, sliced
- 1 pint whipping cream
- 4 cups cooked rice

1. Heat butter in a large skillet over medium high heat.

2. Combine flour, salt, and pepper in a small, shallow bowl; mix well. Roll chicken in flour mixture until pieces are evenly coated.

3. Place coated chicken in skillet and fry until all sides are golden brown. Remove chicken, place on a serving plate, and set aside.

4. Add sliced mushrooms to the pan; sauté until golden brown. Add whipping cream, stir, and cook until golden colored, approximately 20 minutes.

5. Pour sauce over chicken. Serve with white rice on the side.

Veal Casserole

Recipe donated by Herta Carlson
~ SERVES 6

1½ pounds boneless cubed veal
½ cup white wine
2 tablespoons olive oil
1 small onion, peeled and minced
1 clove garlic, minced
2 stalks celery, chopped
1 small green pepper, seeded and chopped
1 carrot, peeled and chopped
2 medium tomatoes, peeled and chopped
½ teaspoon fresh basil
½ teaspoon oregano
1 bay leaf
Salt and pepper to taste
3 cups cooked noodles or white rice

1. Marinate veal in white wine for at least one hour. Drain, reserving wine.

2. Heat olive oil in a large skillet over medium high heat. Add onion and garlic; sauté until soft. Add veal and cook, stirring, until all sides are brown.

3. Add wine, celery, green pepper, carrot, tomatoes, basil, oregano, bay leaf, and salt and pepper to taste. Reduce heat to medium; cover and cook for 30 minutes.

4. Preheat oven to 350 degrees.

5. Transfer stew to 2-quart casserole dish and cover. Bake for one hour or until veal is tender. Serve over noodles or white rice.

Southern Fried Chicken and Gravy

Recipe donated by Michelle Carter

SERVES 4 TO 6

2–3 pound chicken, cut into 8 pieces
2 cups buttermilk or 2 tablespoons vinegar plus enough milk to equal 2 cups, let stand 5 minutes before using
1¼ teaspoons salt
¾ teaspoons black pepper
1 pound lard, vegetable shortening, or combination
1½ cups plus 4 tablespoons flour
1 teaspoon paprika (optional)
1½ teaspoons garlic powder (optional)
2 tablespoons butter
1 cup milk
1 cup boiling water
Salt and black pepper to taste

1. Rinse chicken under cold water and blot dry with paper towels. Combine chicken with buttermilk in a large ceramic bowl. Add ¼ teaspoon salt and ¼ teaspoon black pepper. Stir, cover, and refrigerate for at least 4 hours or overnight.

2. Heat lard in a very large skillet or cast-iron frying pan over medium heat. When lard is melted, the fat should be approximately ½ inch deep in the pan. Oil temperature should reach approximately 365 to 370 degrees.

3. Combine 1½ cups flour, 1 teaspoon salt, and ½ teaspoon pepper in a shallow baking pan. Add paprika and garlic powder if desired. Set aside.

4. Remove chicken from refrigerator; drain buttermilk. Dredge thighs in flour mixture, coating evenly; shake off any excess flour. When the oil reaches 370 degrees, place thighs skin side down in the hottest part of the pan.

5. Dredge breasts in the flour mixture and place in pan, followed by the drumsticks and wings. Chicken pieces should not touch each other. Fry in batches, if necessary. Cover and let chicken fry for 5 minutes. Do not move pieces.

6. Uncover and continue frying for another 8 to 10 minutes. Check the underside by lifting with tongs. Chicken should be a deep golden color. Turn chicken pieces over only once. Replace cover and cook for another 5 minutes.

7. Remove cover and fry for an additional 8 to 10 minutes. When browned on both sides, remove chicken pieces with tongs and place on a flat brown paper bag to drain.

8. To make gravy, pour off all but approximately 3 tablespoons oil from the pan, saving any browned bits with the oil. Over medium high heat, add 2 tablespoons butter and 4 tablespoons flour; whisk well. When mixture is a golden color, add milk and boiling water. Stir vigorously until smooth and the consistency of buttermilk. Add salt and black pepper to taste. Pour into a gravy bowl.

9. Arrange chicken on a platter and serve hot, room temperature, or cold with gravy on the side.

Old–Fashioned Beef Pot Roast

Recipe donated by Bill Coyne
〜 SERVES 6 TO 8

  3 pound boneless beef chuck roast
     Salt and pepper to taste
  2 tablespoons olive oil
  ½ cup water
  6 small onions
  6 small potatoes, peeled and quartered
  6 medium carrots, peeled and sliced in half
  2 tablespoons flour
  1 tablespoon water (enough to make a paste)
 1½ cups water

1. Season the roast with salt and pepper to taste. Heat olive oil in a large Dutch oven over high heat; add roast and brown on both sides. Add ½ cup water. Cover and reduce heat to medium. Braise for approximately 1 hour. Check often, turning roast as needed, and adding additional water if pan is dry.

2. While roast is cooking, remove skins from the onions, but leave top skin intact to hold the onion together. Cut an "x" approximately ½ inch deep at the root end of the onion.

3. Add onions, potatoes, and carrots to the roasting pan after the first hour of cooking. Sprinkle with additional salt and pepper.

4. Continue to braise for an additional hour or until vegetables are tender. Cooking time will be less if vegetables are cut small.

5. Combine flour and 1 tablespoon water in a small bowl to make a paste.

6. Remove vegetables and roast from the pan and cover with foil to keep them warm. Make the gravy. Turn heat to medium high. Add 1½ cups of water and bring to a boil, scraping any brown bits from the bottom of the pan. Cook, stirring, until the sauce is slightly reduced or thickened.

7. While still boiling, gradually add flour paste, whisking vigorously after each addition to prevent lumps. Add enough flour paste to reach desired thickness. Season to taste with additional salt and pepper if needed.

8. Slice the roast. Serve beef and vegetables on a platter, passing gravy separately.

Chicken à la King

Recipe donated by Herta Carlson

SERVES 6

⅓ cup butter or margarine
5 tablespoons flour
½ teaspoon salt
¼ teaspoon pepper
1⅓ cups chicken broth
½ cup light cream
2 cups cooked chicken or turkey, cut into chunks
½ cup pimentos, drained
1 cup peas
1 cup sliced mushrooms
¼ cup dry sherry

1. Melt butter or margarine in the top of a double boiler over hot water. Slowly whisk in flour, salt, and pepper; stir constantly until mixture is smooth.

2. Slowly add chicken broth and cream; stir until hot and slightly thickened.

3. Add cooked chicken or turkey, pimentos, peas, mushrooms, and sherry; stir and let simmer over low heat for approximately 20 minutes.

4. Serve hot over white rice, mashed potatoes, or toast points.

Bomboa's Braised Short Ribs

Recipe donated by Felino Samson
∿ SERVES 4 TO 6

3–4	pounds short ribs
	Salt and pepper to taste
2	carrots, peeled and diced
2	onions, peeled and chopped
2	stalks celery, diced
1	bottle good red wine
1	tablespoon fresh ground black pepper
¼	cup brown sugar
2	quarts veal stock

1. Season short ribs with salt and pepper to taste, then brown over medium high heat in an oven-proof 4-quart casserole dish. Add carrots, onions, and celery. Sweat the vegetables for 1 to 2 minutes. Add red wine and allow to simmer for 5 minutes.

2. Preheat oven to 300 degrees.

3. Add black pepper, brown sugar, and veal stock to casserole dish. Cover and bring to a boil.

4. Place covered casserole in the oven and bake for approximately 2 hours or until meat is tender.

5. Remove ribs and serve. Save braising liquid to drizzle over mashed potatoes or lobster boniato mash (see page 198).

Bomboa's Feijoada

Recipe donated by Felino Samson
SERVES 8 TO 10

4 links spicy pork sausage
1 pound pork shoulder, trimmed and cubed
4 chicken thighs
1 pound beef chuck, trimmed and cubed
1 pound dried black beans, soaked overnight
½ pound dried large white lima beans, soaked overnight
2 medium onions, peeled and chopped
3 large carrots, peeled and diced
4 cloves garlic, chopped
2 stalks celery, diced
2 tablespoons tomato paste
1 cup red wine
2 quarts beef broth
1 bunch leafy kale, chopped
¼ cup farofa (cassava meal)
4 oranges, peeled and sectioned

1. In a large cast iron pot, sear the pork sausage, shoulder, chicken thighs, and beef over medium high heat. Once the meat is seared on all sides, remove from pan and set aside, leaving rendered fat in the pan.

2. Combine the black beans and lima beans in a medium stockpot. Fill with enough water to cover and bring to a boil over medium high heat. Cook until tender. Remove from heat and set aside to cool.

3. Preheat oven to 375 degrees.

4. Place the onions, carrots, garlic, and celery into the cast iron pot. Cook, stirring, over medium heat until tender. Add the tomato paste and stir lightly. Deglaze the pan with red wine. Add the seared meats and bring to a simmer. Once the wine is reduced by half, add the beef stock. Return to a simmer.

Feijoada is the national dish of Brazil. Saturday is traditionally the day to serve this dish since after eating feijoada, going back to work is usually unthinkable. There are many regional variations ranging from a humble dish of meat-flavored beans thickened with abundant cassava meal to this more hearty version with meat, sausage, and chicken. This recipe comes from chef Felino Samson of Bomboa located between Boston's Back Bay and South End.

5. Place the cast iron pot in the oven and bake for approximately 45 minutes or until the meat is tender. Stir in the cooked beans and chopped kale. Bake for an additional 15 minutes, stirring regularly.

6. Remove from oven. Fold in farofa and orange sections, then serve while hot in individual bowls.

Russian Kielbasa

Recipe donated by Dorothy Lysko Brawders
MAKES 4 POUNDS

- 4 pounds pork loin butt (use more, if desired)
- 5 tablespoons salt
- 2 tablespoons dried parsley
- 1 tablespoon pepper
- 1 tablespoon garlic powder
- 3 cups water
- 6 tablespoons mustard seeds
- Sausage casings (frozen until ready to use)

1. Cut meat from bone and slice into small pieces. Run through a meat grinder.

2. Combine salt, parsley, pepper, and garlic powder in a small, tight-lidded jar. Mix well and set aside to use as a combination seasoning.

3. Combine meat, 2½ teaspoons of combination seasoning per pound of meat used, and water in a large mixing bowl. Mix thoroughly by hand until moist. Add mustard seeds and additional water, if needed. Cover and refrigerate overnight.

4. The next day, wash casings in warm water and run cold water through the insides. Tie one end of the casing. Using a sausage funnel, push meat through casing, keeping it firm. Fill entire casing and tie off the other end. Repeat with additional casings until all meat has been used. Kielbasa may be wrapped and refrigerated or frozen until ready to use.

5. To cook, bring water to a boil in a large saucepan. Pierce each kielbasa with a fork to let air bubbles escape, then boil sausages for 45 minutes.

6. Preheat oven to 350 degrees.

7. Remove kielbasa from water and cut into 2-inch sections. Place in rectangular baking pan and bake for 5 to 10 minutes or until slightly brown.

Kapusta

Recipe donated by Jean Rebak Butterfield
🍃 SERVES 8

2–3	pounds pork spareribs (not country style)
	Salt and pepper to taste
1	onion, peeled and coarsely chopped
1	green cabbage, shredded
4	cups sauerkraut, drained and rinsed
2	cups thickly sliced mushrooms
1	cup water
½	cup ketchup
1	bay leaf
1½	pounds kielbasa, cut into 1-inch pieces

1. Preheat oven to 350 degrees.

2. Cut spareribs along the bone with a sharp knife. Season lightly with salt and pepper. Place in a 9 by 13-inch baking pan and bake for 45 minutes or until ribs are completely cooked. Remove ribs from pan, set aside, and reserve approximately 3 tablespoons of drippings.

3. In a large stockpot, heat 3 tablespoons of rib drippings over medium high heat. Add onion and sauté until translucent. Add cabbage, sauerkraut, mushrooms, and water; stir to mix all ingredients well. Add spareribs.

4. Cover pot and simmer for approximately one hour or until cabbage is tender. Stir frequently to prevent burning on the bottom. Add ketchup and stir to coat all ingredients. Add bay leaf.

5. Add kielbasa to the pot. Cook until kielbasa is cooked through, approximately 45 minutes. Remove from heat, cool, and refrigerate overnight.

6. The next day, reheat, remove bay leaf, and serve hot.

Homemade Italian Sausages

Recipe donated by Angelo DeSimone
~&. MAKES 7 POUNDS

6–7 pound boneless Boston butt pork
1 cup dry red wine
1½ teaspoons salt
1 teaspoon black pepper
½ teaspoon crushed red pepper
Sausage casings
1 tablespoon lemon juice

Many flavors and textures may be added to the basic sausage recipe. Add any of the following or a combination in one or two teaspoon increments:

Fennel seeds, ground or whole
Black or green peppercorns, whole, cracked, or coarsely ground
Garlic, whole, half, chopped, or minced
Diced pepper
Chopped onion
Provolone cheese, small cubes
Ground coriander seeds

1. Trim fat from pork with a sharp knife, leaving some fat intact. Run pork through a meat grinder, using a sausage-sized blade, two times; place in a large mixing bowl. Add dry red wine, salt, black pepper, and crushed red pepper flakes. If adding additional filling ingredients, mix in at this time.

2. Make a small patty of the ground pork and fry in a small skillet to test seasonings. Add additional spices to taste, if needed.

3. Cover and marinate in the refrigerator overnight.

4. The next day, soak the sausage casings in cold water and lemon juice.

This is a very simple recipe that goes back three generations. Both my grandparents and parents made these sausages for every special occasion. The recipe originates in southern Italy in a little town just north of Salerno. You can buy the sausage casings from any butcher; have the butcher trim and grind the meat, if desired. Sausages may be prepared many different ways, and they are great on the barbecue. One of our favorite preparation methods is to sauté sausage with several cloves of garlic until brown. Add mushrooms and continue to brown. Add approximately one cup crushed tomatoes, just to color the sauce. Cook until the sausage is cooked through. This variation is wonderful served with a salad and crusty bread.

5. Place a funnel in the mouth of a sausage casing. Stuff with ground pork, making sure not to overfill and split the casing. Twist or tie the sausage into desired lengths using butcher's twine. Poke out any air pockets using a stickpin. Omit pin pricking if using a cheese filling.

6. Sausages may be cooked immediately or wrapped tightly and frozen.

Dried Italian Sausages

Recipe donated by Dorothy DeSimone
MAKES 7 POUNDS

6–7 pound boneless Boston butt pork
1 cup dry red wine
1½ teaspoons salt
1 teaspoon black pepper
½ teaspoon crushed red pepper
Sausage casings
1 tablespoon lemon juice

Many flavors and textures may be added to the basic sausage recipe. Add any of the following or a combination in one or two teaspoon increments:

Fennel seeds, ground or whole
Black or green peppercorns, whole, cracked, or coarsely ground
Garlic, whole, half, chopped, or minced
Diced pepper
Chopped onion
Provolone cheese, small cubes
Ground coriander seeds

1. Trim fat from pork with a sharp knife, leaving some fat intact. Run pork through a meat grinder, using a sausage-sized blade, two times; place in a large mixing bowl. Add dry red wine, salt, black pepper, and crushed red pepper flakes. If adding additional filling ingredients, mix in at this time.

2. Make a small patty of the ground pork and fry in a small skillet to test seasonings. Add additional spices to taste, if needed.

3. Cover and marinate in the refrigerator overnight.

4. The next day, soak the sausage casings in cold water and lemon juice.

5. Place a funnel in the mouth of a sausage casing. Stuff with ground pork, making sure not to overfill and split the casing. Twist and tie the sausage into links every 6 to 7 inches using butcher's twine.

Dried Italian sausages can be pretty tricky to make the first time, but the taste is definitely worth the effort. Since a lot of time is involved, you may double, triple, or quadruple this recipe. In the Northeast, the best time to make these dried sausages is from December to February when the air is dry. Italian families used back hallways, root cellars, attics, sheds, and garages to dry sausages. A good trick for quick pricking: push through 30 stickpins perpendicular to a piece of balsa wood. Tape the pin heads down to the balsa wood with heavy tape. The contraption should resemble a hand brush with several rows. This system works much faster than punching individual holes into the casings.

6. Poke out any air pockets using a stickpin. Prick each sausage link all over to create approximately 90 to 100 stickpin holes.

7. Hang strands of sausages, each approximately 8 links long, in a dry, cool to cold, well-ventilated area. Hang strands where air will circulate around all links. Sausages should not be hung where they will freeze.

8. Every few days, rotate sausages to allow for a more consistent and even drying. Lightly squeeze and wipe sausages with a clean dry cloth to remove moisture, being careful not to apply too much pressure to the links.

9. Dried sausages should be ready to eat in 6 to 8 weeks depending on the weather and the location selected for drying them. Sausages are ready when there is no moisture left and they do not bounce back when pressed with your fingers.

10. Sausages may be eaten immediately or cut into individual links and stored in clean glass jars. Fill each jar with enough olive oil to cover. Store in a cool, dry place for up to 6 months.

Sausages in Cider

Recipe donated by Esme Littleton

~❧ SERVES 6

    1   teaspoon lard or cooking oil
    1   pound pork sausages
    1   large white onion, peeled and sliced in rounds
    1   teaspoon flour
    1   cup cider
    ½   teaspoon salt
    ¼   teaspoon pepper

1. Heat lard or oil in a large skillet over medium high heat. Reduce heat to medium, add sausages, and brown on all sides. Remove sausages from pan and set aside; leave fat in pan.

2. Add onion slices and sauté in fat from sausages until soft and light brown. When done, remove all but about one teaspoonful of fat from the pan. Whisk flour into the remaining fat. Add additional flour, if needed. There should be enough flour to absorb the fat.

3. Add cider and stir until sauce comes to a boil. Season with salt and pepper. Return sausages to the pan.

4. Cover and cook for 15 minutes. Serve while hot.

Bob the Chef's Jambalaya

Recipe donated by Darryl Settles
SERVES 6

Thelma Callender-Burns takes a moment to discuss recipes with Darryl Settles, owner of Bob the Chef's located in Boston's South End. There is a special connection for Ms. Callender-Burns because her daughter worked at the restaurant.

¼ pound butter or margarine
1 pound smoked beef sausages
1 cup chopped onions
1 cup chopped celery
½ cup diced red pepper
1 pound boneless chicken, diced
1 cup chopped tomatoes
1 pound shrimp, peeled and diced
1 tablespoon crushed red pepper
2 tablespoons Cajun seasoning
1 cup tomato puree
2 cups rice
¼ cup dry chicken base
2 cups water

1. Melt butter or margarine in a large skillet over medium high heat. Add sausages, onions, celery, red pepper, and chicken. Sauté for 10 to 15 minutes. Add tomatoes, shrimp, crushed red pepper, Cajun seasoning, and tomato puree; stir and continue to cook for 5 minutes.

2. Add rice; stir until mixed well.

3. Add chicken base and water, then cover and boil for 20 to 25 minutes. Most of the water should be absorbed, but the rice should still be a little moist.

4. Serve hot in individual bowls.

Stuffed Cabbage

Recipe donated by Casimir Szmaj
SERVES 6 TO 8

1 cup white rice
1 large head cabbage
2 teaspoons salt
2 tablespoons butter
1 medium onion, peeled and chopped
1 pound ground beef
½ teaspoon pepper
3 cups tomato sauce

This old Polish staple has been a favorite for many years. The original recipe calls for fresh tomato sauce; however, the American rendition is usually made with canned condensed tomato soup. For the sweeter American flavor, stir approximately 2 tablespoons of brown sugar into the tomato sauce before pouring it over the rolls.

1. Bring 2 cups of water to a boil in a medium saucepan. Add rice, then cover and cook until done, about 20 minutes. Set aside to cool.

2. Core the cabbage and place in a small stockpot with 2 cups water and 1 teaspoon salt. Bring to a boil over high heat. Cut or pull off cabbage leaves as they become wilted. Trim the thick center vein off each leaf with a knife.

3. Melt butter in a medium skillet over medium high heat. Add onion and sauté until golden brown. Remove from heat and set aside.

4. Combine fresh ground beef, cooked rice, onion, salt, and pepper in a medium-sized mixing bowl; mix well with hands.

5. Preheat oven to 350 degrees.

6. To assemble, start with a cabbage leaf under-side up, then place approximately two tablespoons of filling across the stem end. Turn up the stem and fold over the sides, rolling tightly to form a bulky cigar shape; repeat process with additional cabbage leaves until all filling is used.

7. Line the bottom of a 9 by 13-inch baking pan with one layer of cabbage rolls. Top with half the tomato sauce. Add a second layer of cabbage rolls and top with the remaining tomato sauce. Bake for 1½ hours. Serve hot.

Ham Balls

Recipe donated by Joan Able

☙ SERVES 6 TO 8

This may also be served as an appetizer. Instead of forming into loaves, form mixture into golf balls.

1½ pounds ham, ground or finely diced

1 pound lean pork, ground or finely diced

2 cups dry breadcrumbs

2 eggs, well beaten

1 cup milk

Sauce:

1 cup brown sugar

1 tablespoon dry mustard

⅜ cup vinegar

½ cup water

1. Preheat oven to 325 degrees.

2. Hand mix ham, pork, breadcrumbs, eggs, and milk in a large mixing bowl. Form into small, firm loaves, approximately 2 inches by 3 inches. Arrange in a 9 by 13-inch baking pan, making sure sides of loaves do not touch.

3. Combine brown sugar, dry mustard, vinegar, and water in a medium-sized mixing bowl; mix well. Ladle sauce evenly over the ham loaves.

4. Place in oven and bake for 1½ hours.

Pastichio

Recipe donated by Amy Salvo

SERVES 8

 1 tablespoon vegetable oil
 1 onion, peeled and grated
 1½ pounds ground chuck
 ½ teaspoon pepper
 1 teaspoon salt
 ¼ teaspoon cinnamon
 ¼ teaspoon allspice
 1 cup water
 2 tablespoons tomato sauce
 1 pound thin macaroni
 5½ cups whole milk
 4 tablespoons butter
 9 tablespoons cornstarch
 5 eggs, beaten
 1 cup grated Romano cheese

1. Heat vegetable oil in a large skillet over medium heat. Add onion and brown lightly. Add ground chuck, pepper, salt, cinnamon, and allspice; stir and cook until meat is brown and loose. Add water and tomato sauce. Cover and cook until water is absorbed.

2. Cook macaroni according to package directions. Drain when done.

3. Preheat oven to 350 degrees.

4. Heat 5 cups milk in a medium saucepan over medium heat. Add butter and stir.

5. Dissolve cornstarch in a small cup with remaining ½ cup milk. Add to saucepan with milk and butter. Whisk briskly until mixture is thick and begins to boil. Remove from heat and set aside to cool for 10 minutes. Add eggs; mix until smooth and creamy.

6. Place half of the macaroni in a 9 by 13-inch baking pan. Sprinkle half the Romano cheese on top and toss. Layer ground chuck mixture on top of macaroni. Toss the remaining macaroni and Romano cheese; layer over the ground chuck. Ladle cream sauce evenly over the entire dish, making sure the top macaroni layer is immersed in sauce.

7. Bake for approximately one hour, until top is light brown. Allow to cool and set for a few minutes before serving.

Carmella's Chicken

Recipe donated by Carmella D'Agostino
~🌶 SERVES 4

½	cup vegetable oil
⅓	cup soy sauce
1	teaspoon ginger
1	tablespoon lemon juice
1	clove garlic, finely chopped
½	teaspoon salt
½	teaspoon pepper
3½–4	pound whole chicken, cut into pieces

1. Combine vegetable oil, soy sauce, ginger, lemon juice, garlic, salt, and pepper in a large mixing bowl; mix well.

2. Wash pieces of chicken in warm water and towel dry. Place chicken in marinade, cover, and shake well to ensure that all chicken pieces are covered. Refrigerate for at least 4 hours or overnight.

3. Preheat oven to 350 degrees.

4. Place chicken pieces skin-side down in a 9 by 13-inch baking pan and bake for 30 minutes. After 30 minutes, turn chicken pieces over, increase heat to 450 degrees, and bake for an additional 30 minutes. Serve while hot.

Rose Chicken with Mushrooms

You can add just about anything you like to the stuffing, including giblets or some celery. The sour cream adds a nice color to the chicken skin.

Recipe donated by Frida Levzerovich
SERVES 4

3½–4	pound whole chicken
1	pound fresh mushrooms, sliced
1½	cups fresh breadcrumbs
	Salt and pepper to taste
1	tablespoon lemon juice
1	teaspoon salt
½	teaspoon pepper
¼	cup sour cream

1. Preheat oven to 350 degrees.

2. Wash chicken in warm water and towel dry.

3. Combine mushrooms and breadcrumbs in a small mixing bowl. Add salt and pepper to taste; mix well.

4. Brush inside of chicken with lemon juice. Stuff chicken with mushrooms and breadcrumbs, then tie legs shut with kitchen twine. Season outside of chicken with salt and pepper. Brush chicken skin generously with sour cream.

5. Bake for 1½ hours or until the skin is rose-colored and the chicken is cooked through .

German Meatballs

Recipe donated by Ruth Austin

SERVES 8

    1   bread slice, cut 1 inch thick
    ½   pound veal
    ½   pound beef
    ½   pound lean pork
    2   eggs, well beaten
    5   cups vegetable or beef stock
    1   tablespoon butter
    ¼   cup finely chopped onion
    3   tablespoons fresh chopped parsley
 1¼   teaspoon salt
    ¼   teaspoon paprika
    ½   teaspoon grated lemon rind
    1   teaspoon lemon juice
    1   teaspoon Worcestershire sauce

Gravy:
    ¼   pound butter
    ¾   cup flour
    ¼   teaspoon paprika
        Salt and pepper to taste
    2   tablespoons capers

1. Place bread slice in a small bowl with water to cover. Set aside and let soak.

2. Run veal, beef, and pork through a meat grinder two times. Place in a large mixing bowl. Add eggs and mix well.

3. Heat vegetable or beef stock in a large saucepan over medium high heat.

4. Melt 1 tablespoon butter in a small saucepan over medium high heat. Add chopped onion. Sauté until onion is brown. Add onion to meat mixture.

5. Press water out of bread with hands and add to meat. Add parsley, salt, paprika, grated lemon rind, lemon juice, and Worcestershire sauce; mix well with hands.

6. Roll into balls approximately 1 to 2 inches thick. Drop balls into saucepan with simmering stock. Cover, reduce heat to low, and simmer for 15 minutes. Remove meatballs from the stock and set aside.

7. Make the gravy by adding butter to the remaining stock. Increase heat to medium high and slowly whisk in flour until smooth. Add paprika and salt and pepper to taste. Bring to a boil while whisking vigorously. When gravy is smooth, stir in capers. Reduce heat to low, add meatballs to gravy, and stir.

8. Serve hot with rice or broad egg noodles on the side.

Baked Kibbee

Recipe donated by Lorraine David Maloof
 SERVES 8

Kibbee:
- 1½ cups burghul wheat
- 2 small onions, peeled
- 2 pounds fine-ground lamb
- 1 teaspoon salt
- 1 teaspoon Syrian pepper
- 2 tablespoons rendered butter or vegetable oil for brushing

Stuffing—Hushwee:
- ¼ cup pine nuts
- 2 tablespoons rendered butter
- 1 pound course-ground lamb or beef
- 1 medium onion, finely chopped
- ½ teaspoon Syrian pepper
- Salt and black pepper to taste

1. Wash burghul wheat, add water to cover, and soak for approximately 30 minutes. Squeeze thoroughly with a towel to remove excess water.

2. Puree onions in food processor.

3. Make kibbee in a large mixing bowl by combining lamb, burghul wheat, onions, salt, and Syrian pepper. Mix well by hand, dipping hands in a bowl of ice water to keep mixture moist while thoroughly blending. Set aside.

4. To make stuffing, sauté pine nuts in a large skillet with rendered butter until light brown. Add lamb or beef, onion, Syrian pepper, and salt and pepper to taste. Cook until meat is brown. Set aside.

5. Preheat oven to 350 degrees. For slow cooking, set oven to 250 degrees.

6. Grease a 9 by 13-inch baking pan. Spread half the kibbee mixture over the bottom of the pan. Press down firmly with fingers to make sure the first layer

is set tight. Spread the stuffing on top of the first layer and top with the remaining kibbee mixture. Moisten hands with ice water to smooth out the top.

7. Cut the top layer of the kibbee into diamond shapes with a knife. Dot kibbee with butter or brush a thin layer of oil over the top. Pierce the center of each diamond about half way through with the tip of a small knife so the butter or oil will penetrate.

8. Place dish on the top shelf of the oven and bake at 350 degrees for 15 minutes. Move to the bottom shelf and bake for 15 minutes. Return to the top shelf and bake until top is brown and edges are well cooked, about 10 to 15 minutes more. Oil may splash out of the pan during cooking. If you prefer, set the oven to 250 degrees and cook for approximately 1½ hours to avoid any oil splashing.

9. Remove from oven and serve while hot with fresh yogurt on the side and a side salad or rice pilaf,.

Chicken with Butter Honey Sauce

Recipe donated by Jim Poutre

~ SERVES 4

- ¼ pound butter
- 1 cup flour
- 2 teaspoons salt
- ¼ teaspoon pepper
- 2 teaspoons paprika
- 1 frying chicken, cut into pieces

Butter Honey Sauce:

- 4 tablespoons butter
- ¼ cup honey
- ¼ cup lemon juice

1. Preheat oven to 400 degrees.

2. Melt ¼ pound butter in a 9 by 13-inch baking pan in the oven.

3. Combine flour, salt, pepper, and paprika in a shallow bowl; mix well. Place chicken pieces into mixture, coating evenly on all sides.

4. Remove pan from oven when butter is melted. Add chicken to pan, turning to coat both sides with butter. Bake chicken, skin-side down, for 30 minutes. After 30 minutes, turn chicken skin-side up.

5. Make butter honey sauce by melting butter in a small saucepan over medium heat. Add honey and lemon juice and stir until smooth. Pour sauce over chicken and bake for 15 minutes. Baste with sauce and bake for an additional 15 minutes or until chicken is cooked through.

Chicken Rolitini

Recipe donated by Barbara Massetti
∾ SERVES 6 TO 8

1	pound bacon
6–8	thinly sliced chicken cutlets
1	8-ounce brick cream cheese, softened
½	cup chopped scallions

1. Partially cook bacon in a large skillet until fat is rendered. Remove bacon and set on paper towels to drain.

2. Pound chicken cutlets between two sheets of waxed paper with a meat pounder until thin. Set aside.

3. Preheat oven to 375 degrees.

4. Combine cream cheese and scallions in a small mixing bowl; mix well.

5. Lay cutlets flat on a clean work surface. Place approximately 2 tablespoons cream cheese mixture in the middle of each cutlet. Roll each cutlet up from the bottom into a cylinder shape. Wrap 3 slices of partially cooked bacon around each cutlet and secure with toothpicks.

6. Place cutlets on an ungreased baking pan and bake for 35 to 40 minutes, or until bacon is crisp and cream cheese is bubbling. Allow to cool for a few minutes before serving.

Beef with Prunes

Recipe donated by Sofia Simkina
SERVES 6

2	tablespoons vegetable oil
2	large white onions, peeled and sliced
2½	pounds beef chuck, cut into 2-inch cubes
6	bay leaves
1	cup water
1	teaspoon salt
1	teaspoon pepper
½	pound prunes, pitted

1. Heat vegetable oil in a large skillet over medium high heat. Add onions and sauté approximately 5 minutes. Add beef and cook, stirring, until all sides are brown.

2. Add bay leaves, water, salt, and pepper. Reduce heat to low, cover, and simmer for approximately 40 minutes.

3. Add prunes and stir. Cover and simmer for an additional hour. Serve hot with rice, noodles, or mashed potatoes.

Jacob Wirth's Cider Pork Chops with Maple Glaze

Recipe donated by Phyllis Kaplowitz

SERVES 4

- 2 cups beer
- 2 cups apple cider
- 1 cup water
- ¼ cup kosher salt
- ¼ cup brown sugar
- 2 cinnamon sticks
- 2 tablespoons vanilla
- 2 tablespoons thyme
- 4 center cut pork chops, 1½ inch thick, bone in or boneless
- 2 tablespoons vegetable oil

Glaze:
- ¾ cup maple syrup
- ½ cup dry white wine
- ⅓ cup Dijon style mustard

1. Combine beer, cider, water, kosher salt, brown sugar, cinnamon sticks, vanilla, and thyme in a large stockpot. Bring to a boil. Once brine begins to boil, remove from heat to cool. Cover and refrigerate until chilled.

2. When brine is chilled, submerge pork chops in stockpot, cover tightly, and refrigerate for at least 24 hours.

3. Heat oil in a large skillet over high heat. Remove pork from brine, pat dry, and place pork into skillet. Cook each side until brown.

4. Combine maple syrup and white wine in a medium saucepan and bring to a boil over high heat. Whisk in Dijon mustard and stir until smooth.

5. Place pork chops on a serving plate and spoon maple syrup glaze on top.

Marsico Family Meatballs and Sauce

Recipe donated by George Schiavone

SERVES 6 TO 8

Meatballs:

      2 pounds lean ground chuck
      1 cup seasoned dry breadcrumbs
    ¾ cup finely grated Romano cheese
      2 large eggs, lightly beaten
      5 cloves garlic, diced
    1¼ teaspoons dried basil
      1 bunch fresh parsley, chopped
         Salt and pepper to taste
    ⅜ cup water

Sauce:

    ½ cup olive oil
      1 large yellow or white onion, peeled and finely chopped
    6–8 garlic cloves, finely chopped
    10 links sweet Italian sausage with fennel seeds
  10½ cups tomato puree
    1½ cups tomato paste
    1½ cups water
      2 tablespoons dried parsley
      1 tablespoon dried basil
      1 teaspoon dried oregano
         Salt and pepper to taste
    2–3 bay leaves, split into pieces

1. Combine ground chuck, breadcrumbs, Romano cheese, eggs, garlic, basil, parsley, and salt and pepper to taste in a large mixing bowl. Add water and hand mix until well blended. Shape into meatballs approximately 1½ inches in diameter.

My Neapolitan grandmother, Lucia Parziale Marsico, always insisted on sausages with fennel seeds to give this Italian staple a unique taste. For a hot and spicy sauce, replace sweet sausages with hot sausages and add a few dry chili peppers to the sauce. For our family ritual, my mom always split the bay leaf into three pieces because there were three of us in my family, my mom, dad, and myself. My grandmother reverently split the bay leaf into eight pieces for two parents and six children.

2. Make sauce by heating olive oil in a large stockpot over medium high heat. When oil is hot, reduce heat to medium and add onion and garlic; stir until onion is soft and garlic is light brown.

3. Brown sausages and meatballs in batches. When done, place all meatballs and sausages into the stockpot.

4. Add tomato puree, tomato paste, water, parsley, basil, oregano, and salt and pepper to taste. Place one bay leaf on top.

5. Simmer uncovered for at least two hours, adding additional water as needed. Replace the bay leaf after one hour. Serve over fresh cooked pasta.

Pork with Hominy and Greens

Recipe donated by Leo Romero

~ SERVES 6

6	pork cubed steaks
⅓	cup flour
¼	cup vegetable oil
1	onion, peeled and chopped
2	slices bacon, cut up
1	cup beef broth
1	pound turnip or beet greens, chopped
1	20-ounce can hominy
2	tomatoes, chopped
1	tablespoon chili powder
1	tablespoon white vinegar
½	teaspoon salt
½	teaspoon cumin
½	teaspoon oregano
¼	teaspoon black pepper
	Chopped onion or fresh cilantro for garnish (optional)

1. Coat both sides of pork steaks lightly in flour.

2. Heat vegetable oil in a four-quart Dutch oven over high heat. Reduce heat to medium, add pork steaks, and cook until brown on both sides. Remove from pan and drain on paper towels.

3. Add onion and bacon to the Dutch oven; stir and cook until tender. Add broth, turnip or beet greens, hominy, tomatoes, chili powder, vinegar, salt, cumin, oregano, and pepper; cook, stirring well, over high heat.

4. Place pork on top, return to a boil, then reduce heat to low. Cover and simmer until pork is tender, approximately 30 minutes.

5. Place pork and hominy on a plate and garnish with chopped onion or fresh cilantro if desired.

Barbecue Sauce and Spareribs

Recipe donated by Hyacinth Singletary

SERVES 4 TO 6

- 1 cup soy sauce
- 1 cup water
- 6 tablespoons brown sugar
- 4 teaspoons ginger root, finely grated
- 4 teaspoons vegetable oil
- 4 teaspoons vinegar
- 2 teaspoons garlic, finely chopped
- ¼ teaspoon red pepper
- 6 pounds pork spareribs

1. Make barbecue sauce by combining soy sauce, water, brown sugar, ginger root, vegetable oil, vinegar, garlic, and red pepper in a medium mixing bowl; mix well.

2. Place ribs in a large, rectangular baking pan and generously spread barbecue sauce over ribs. Cover tightly with aluminum foil, refrigerate, and marinate for at least 4 hours or overnight.

3. Preheat oven to 350 degrees.

4. Keep ribs covered with aluminum foil and bake for 45 minutes. Remove from the oven and allow to cool before serving.

Sweet and Sour Pork

Recipe donated by Esme Littleton
SERVES 4

Sauce:

- 1 tablespoon vegetable oil
- 1 carrot, peeled and shredded
- 2 onions, peeled and shredded
- ½ cup pineapple chunks
- 3 tablespoons soy sauce
- 2 tablespoons sugar
- ½ cup pineapple juice
- 1 tablespoon cornstarch
- 1 teaspoon water
- 2 tablespoons vinegar
- ½ teaspoon salt

- ½ cup vegetable oil for deep frying
- 1 pound pork, cut into pieces
- 2 tablespoons flour
- 2 eggs
- 2 tablespoons cornstarch
- 3 cups white rice, cooked

Esme Littleton chats with Jean-Jean "JJ" Jules, chef at Legal Sea Food. Ms. Littleton was born in Sri Lanka and moved to Boston in 1967. She's always had a great love for cooking and has compiled recipes from around the world. One interesting tidbit is that Ms. Littleton was one of the first employees of Central Boston Elder Services—she even made the opening celebration cake.

1. Make the sauce by heating 1 tablespoon vegetable oil in a medium saucepan over medium high heat. Add carrot and onions; mix well. Add pineapple chunks and cook for approximately 10 minutes, stirring regularly. Add soy sauce, sugar, and pineapple juice; stir and simmer for 15 minutes.

2. Mix cornstarch with water in a small bowl. Add to the sauce. Stir and bring to a boil; add vinegar and season with salt to taste.

3. Heat two tablespoons oil in a large skillet over medium high heat. Add pork and fry all sides until cooked. Remove from pan and set aside.

4. Combine flour, eggs, and cornstarch in a small mixing bowl; mix until smooth. Put aside to let set.

5. Add remaining oil to skillet in which pork was browned, then heat over medium high heat.

6. Coat pork pieces evenly on all sides in the flour, cornstarch, and egg mixture. Fry coated pork pieces in oil over medium heat until golden brown on all sides. Remove pork with a slotted spoon and set on paper towels to drain.

7. Place pork on a serving plate. Ladle pineapple sauce over the pork and serve with white rice on the side.

Gert's Meat Pie

Recipe donated by Edward A. Bielecki

SERVES 4 TO 6

- 1 pound lean ground beef
- ½ teaspoon garlic powder
- ½ teaspoon salt
- 1 cup dry breadcrumbs
- ½ cup milk
- ¼ cup tomato sauce
- ¼ cup sliced mushrooms
- ¼ cup shredded mozzarella cheese
- ¼ teaspoon oregano
- 2 tablespoons grated Parmesan or Romano cheese

1. Preheat oven to 400 degrees.

2. Combine ground beef, garlic powder, salt, breadcrumbs, and milk in a medium mixing bowl. Press mixture into a 9-inch pie pan.

3. Spread tomato sauce over the meat mixture. Sprinkle mushrooms on top. Spread mozzarella cheese over the mushrooms. Sprinkle with oregano and top with Parmesan or Romano cheese.

4. Bake for approximately 20 minutes. Allow to cool for a few minutes. Cut into slices and serve hot.

Tortiere

Recipe donated by Almeda Poutre

❧ MAKES 2 MEAT PIES

- 2 pounds lean ground pork
- 1 pound lean ground beef
- 2 large white onions, peeled and chopped
- 1 clove garlic, chopped
- 1 teaspoon poultry seasoning
- 2 teaspoons salt
- 1 teaspoon celery salt
- 2 teaspoons black pepper
- 1 teaspoon sage
- 3 teaspoons cinnamon
- ½ teaspoon cloves
- 2 cups water
- 3 medium potatoes, peeled, boiled, and lightly mashed
- 2 pastry pie shells, tops and bottoms, see page 235 for recipe

Tortiere is French for meat pie. This recipe is traditionally served on Christmas Eve following midnight services at church. Our family also serves this as a Thanksgiving side dish with turkey without using the pastry shells. Pies may also be made in advance and frozen. Prepare as directed without baking. Wrap tightly and freeze. When ready to serve, allow pie to thaw before baking.

1. Combine pork, beef, and onions in a large cast iron skillet. Cook over medium heat until meat is no longer pink. Stir in garlic, poultry seasoning, salt, celery salt, black pepper, sage, cinnamon, cloves, and water.

2. Cover and simmer for 20 minutes. Uncover and allow to simmer for an additional 10 minutes. Fold in mashed potatoes, remove from heat, and allow filling to cool.

3. Preheat oven to 425 degrees.

4. Prepare pie shells. Each pie should have a bottom and top crust. Divide meat filling between the two pies. Cover each pie with the top crust and pinch shut. Make a few slits on the top crust of each pie with a knife to allow air to escape.

5. Bake for 15 minutes. Reduce oven temperature to 350 degrees and cook for an additional 25 minutes. Allow to cool for a few minutes before serving.

Spinach Meatloaf

Recipe donated by Virginia Korpal
SERVES 6

1¼ pounds lean ground beef
10 ounces chopped spinach, fresh or frozen (defrosted)
1 egg, lightly beaten
¾ cup dry breadcrumbs
⅛ cup freshly grated Parmesan cheese
1 clove garlic, finely chopped
1 teaspoon chopped parsley
½ teaspoon salt
½ teaspoon pepper

Sauce:
2 tablespoons olive oil
1 white onion, peeled and sliced
1 teaspoon chopped parsley
6 tomatoes, peeled and chopped with juices (14 ounces canned tomatoes will work also)
2½ tablespoons brown sugar
1 teaspoon pepper

1. Preheat oven to 325 degrees.

2. Combine ground beef, spinach, egg, breadcrumbs, Parmesan cheese, garlic, parsley, salt, and pepper in a large mixing bowl. Mix by hand and form into a rectangular loaf approximately 4 by 8-inches. Place in a loaf pan or small rectangular baking dish.

3. Bake for one hour and 15 minutes.

4. Heat olive oil in a large skillet over medium heat. Add onion and sauté until tender. Add parsley, tomatoes, brown sugar, and pepper and stir until combined. Allow sauce to simmer for approximately 15 to 20 minutes, stirring occasionally.

5. Remove from oven and let cool for a few minutes. Slice and ladle tomato sauce over the top. Serve with mashed potatoes.

Edythe Mae's Meatloaf

Recipe donated by Edythe Mae David

SERVES 6

- 1¾ pounds lean ground beef
- ¾ cup dry breadcrumbs
- ¾ cup applesauce
- 6 tablespoons ketchup
- 1 egg, lightly beaten
- ¾ teaspoon salt
- ¼ teaspoon sage

1. Preheat oven to 350 degrees.

2. Combine ground beef, breadcrumbs, applesauce, ketchup, egg, salt, and sage in a medium-sized mixing bowl. Mix well by hand and form into a 6-inch square loaf. Place loaf in a small square or rectangular baking pan. Bake for 50 minutes.

3. Remove meatloaf from oven and allow to cool for a few minutes before serving. Serve with mashed potatoes.

Beef Bracioletinne

Recipe donated by Barbara Cedrone Horan
SERVES 4 TO 6

Breadcrumb Mixture:

 1 cup fresh breadcrumbs
½ teaspoon salt
½ teaspoon pepper
½ cup Parmesan cheese
¼ teaspoon garlic salt

1½ pounds top round sandwich steaks (approximately 10 steaks), cut against the grain
10 slices prosciutto, thin
10 slices Swiss cheese, thin
 3 tablespoons vegetable or olive oil
 2 cups fresh mushrooms, sliced
½ cup sweet Marsala wine

1. Make breadcrumb mixture by combining breadcrumbs, salt, pepper, Parmesan cheese, and garlic salt in a medium-sized bowl. Set aside.

2. Trim fat from sandwich steaks, place each between two pieces of waxed paper, and pound to approximately ¼ inch thick.

3. Place pounded steaks flat on a large work surface. Top each steak with one slice of prosciutto, one slice of Swiss cheese, and one tablespoon of the breadcrumb mixture. Roll each strip from the bottom up and tuck in ends to ensure stuffing does not drip out. Tie each meat roll around the middle then crisscross with kitchen twine.

4. Heat vegetable or olive oil in a large skillet over medium high heat. Reduce heat to medium low and completely brown each roll on all sides. Remove meat rolls from pan and set aside.

5. Drain all but about one tablespoon of oil and drippings from the pan. Add mushrooms and sauté until cooked. Add Marsala wine and cook for about three minutes.

6. Remove string from meat rolls and return to pan to warm. Serve hot.

Steak Pizzaiola

Recipe donated by Lidia Maria Dieramo

SERVES 2

¼ cup olive oil
2 sirloin steaks (6 ounces each), cut approximately ½ inch thick
3 cloves garlic, finely chopped
1 bunch fresh basil, chopped
½ teaspoon salt
¼ teaspoon pepper
1¼ cups fresh tomatoes, peeled and chopped

1. Preheat oven to 350 degrees.

2. Place ⅛ cup olive oil in a roasting pan large enough to fit steaks side by side and evenly coat the bottom. Place sirloin steaks in pan and top with garlic, basil, salt, and pepper.

3. Pour chopped tomatoes over steaks and top with the remaining olive oil. Bake for 30 minutes for rare, or approximately 45 minutes for medium.

M.J. O'Connor's Stuffed Irish Boxty

Recipe donated by Ray Gardiner

⌒⌒ SERVES 4

1½ pounds potatoes, peeled and shredded
1   white onion, peeled and shredded
3   cups whole milk
4   large eggs
4   tablespoons butter, melted
1   teaspoon tarragon
1   teaspoon salt
1   teaspoon black pepper
3   cups flour
1½ tablespoons lemon juice
1   teaspoon fresh chopped dill
1   tablespoon parsley flakes
¼   cup vegetable oil

Cheddar Sauce:
1   cup butter
½   white onion, peeled and finely chopped
½   carrot, peeled and finely chopped
1   celery rib, finely diced
1   cup flour
1   bay leaf
1   quart whole milk
¾   pound cheddar cheese, grated
½   teaspoon salt
1   teaspoon pepper

1. Squeeze potatoes with a cloth towel or paper towels to soak up excess liquid and set aside.

2. Mix together the milk, eggs, melted butter, tarragon, salt, and pepper in a large bowl. Add the potatoes and onion.

3. Thicken the mixture with flour. Add lemon juice, dill, and parsley. Mix until smooth.

4. Heat two tablespoons of oil in a medium skillet over medium heat. Pour 8 ounces of batter into pan and cook for approximately 4 to 5 minutes.

This is an Irish dish that is very flexible as a main course. You may use leftovers or just about anything you have on hand to stuff the boxty. Ham and cheese, chicken stew, or turkey, chopped celery, and mayonnaise are a few family favorites. Just heat up the filling and stuff inside the boxty.

5. Flip boxty over to cook the other side. Top half the boxty with any variety of cooked meats, cheeses, or stews. Cook for another 4 to 5 minutes, then flip omelet style. Cook until filling is warm. Repeat until all potato batter is used. Use additional vegetable oil as needed. Boxty may be stored in a warm oven until all are ready to serve.

6. Make the sauce by melting the butter in a large stockpot over medium heat. Add the onion, carrot, and celery and sauté until soft. Slowly stir in flour and add the bay leaf. Reduce heat and cook for 5 minutes.

7. Increase the heat to medium and slowly add the milk, stirring constantly. Remove from heat, then stir in cheddar cheese, salt, and pepper.

8. To serve, place stuffed boxty on a plate and top with hot cheddar sauce.

Spedini

Recipe donated by Salvatore Scamardo
~🕊 SERVES 4 TO 6

- 3 yellow onions, peeled
- 2 pounds lean sirloin (you can also use Braciola meat purchased from any butcher)
- 2¼ cups dry breadcrumbs
- 1½ teaspoons Italian seasoning
- 2 cups fresh grated Parmesan cheese
- ¾ cup tomato paste (6-ounce can)
- ½ cup olive oil
- 24 bay leaves
- Salt and pepper to taste
- 6 wood or metal 8-inch long skewers

1. Boil onions in a small saucepan in 2 cups water until soft and translucent. Drain and set aside to cool.

2. Trim any fat from the meat and pound between two pieces of waxed paper to ¼ inch thickness . Cut sirloin into 2 by 5-inch wide strips, yielding approximately 36 strips. Set aside.

3. Mix 2 cups breadcrumbs, 1 teaspoon Italian seasoning, and ½ cup grated Parmesan cheese in a shallow bowl or pan. Set aside.

4. Once onions are cool, finely chop one onion. Combine chopped onion, remaining ¼ cup breadcrumbs, remaining ½ teaspoon Italian seasoning, remaining 1½ cups Parmesan cheese, and tomato paste in a medium-sized mixing bowl and stir until paste-like consistency is achieved.

5. Pour olive oil in shallow bowl. Dip each strip of beef in the olive oil, then dip in the breadcrumb and Parmesan mixture, making sure both sides are coated. Set the breaded strips aside. Do not dispose of olive oil.

6. Quarter the remaining onions with a sharp knife and place in a small bowl.

This delicious recipe comes from my father, Pasquale. He brought it over from his hometown of San Giuseppe Jato, Sicily, Italy. It is usually served at special occasions. Many variations of this dish exist, but this version is very tender, flavorful, and aromatic. It is a delicious—some say addictive—dish that your guests will ask for again and again.

7. Lay several pieces of breaded sirloin on a clean work surface, assembly-line fashion. Smooth approximately 1 teaspoon of the chopped onion and tomato paste mixture onto each strip. Roll each strip up vertically and set aside. Continue process until all strips have been filled and rolled.

8. Preheat oven to 450 degrees and set oven rack to lower broiler rack position.

9. Skewer an onion quarter, then one rolled meat strip followed by one bay leaf. Repeat this sequence until there are 6 rolled meat strips on each skewer.

10. Place skewers onto a broiling pan and brush generously with olive oil.

11. Broil for 6 minutes on each side or until crispy brown. Allow to cool for several minutes before serving.

Polenta All'Uccelletto

Recipe donated by Marisa N. Oliveri
SERVES 6

- 8 tablespoons olive oil
- 6 cloves garlic, chopped
- 1 6-ounce can tomato paste
- 5 cups water
- 1 pound Italian sausages
- 2 cups black olives, pitted
- 1 tablespoon sage
- ½ pound cornmeal
- ¼ cup grated Romano cheese
- Salt and pepper to taste

1. Heat olive oil in a medium stockpot over medium high heat. Reduce heat to medium. Add garlic, sauté until golden brown. Add tomato paste and 1 cup of water. Reduce heat to low and simmer for 30 minutes, stirring occasionally.

2. Add sausages, olives, and sage. Cover and cook for one hour.

3. Bring remaining 4 cups water to a boil in a separate medium-sized stockpot over high heat. Add cornmeal and cook for 30 minutes, stirring constantly. Add more water if necessary.

4. Place cornmeal on a serving tray or pan. Top with sausages, gravy, and olives. Sprinkle with Romano cheese and salt and pepper to taste. Serve while hot.

Pasta with Pesto Sauce

Recipe donated by Jennie DiFillippo
✎ SERVES 4 TO 6

- 2 cups fresh basil leaves
- 3 tablespoons chopped fresh Italian parsley
- ½ cup extra-virgin olive oil
- 2 tablespoons pine nuts
- 2 cloves garlic
- 1 teaspoon salt
- ½ cup fresh-grated Parmesan cheese
- 3 tablespoons fresh-grated Romano cheese
- 3 tablespoons unsalted butter, softened
- 1 pound pasta
- 1 tablespoon black pepper for garnish
- 1 tablespoon toasted pine nuts for garnish
  Fresh-grated cheese

This recipe comes from Steve DiFillippo's mother. Steve is the owner of the Davio's restaurants in Boston and Cambridge. They make large quantities of fresh pesto sauce when the basil leaves are fresh and available and freeze it so it lasts throughout the year. If freezing pesto, do not add the Parmesan and Romano cheeses or the butter. Defrost completely, while covered, to room temperature. Transfer to a bowl and toss in the cheeses and butter.

1. Wash basil leaves under water and dry with a cloth or in a salad spinner.

2. Combine basil leaves, Italian parsley, olive oil, pine nuts, garlic, and salt in a blender or food processor; pulse until mixture is smooth. Transfer to a medium-sized mixing bowl.

3. Using a wooden spoon, mix in the Parmesan and Romano cheeses. Add butter and mix well. Pesto sauce is ready to serve.

4. If tossing with pasta, prepare pasta according to directions on the package. Drain the pasta, saving approximately ½ cup pasta water.

5. Place cooked pasta in a bowl. Top with pesto sauce. Add 1 to 2 tablespoons of the hot pasta water and lightly toss. If sauce is too thick, add more pasta water.

6. Serve, garnished with black pepper, toasted pine nuts, and fresh grated cheese.

Djaj Bi Hashwee

Recipe donated by Lorraine David Maloof

SERVES 8 TO 10

- 2 small chickens or 1 large chicken
- 2 cups cold water
  - Salt and pepper to taste
- 1 tablespoon oil
- ½ cup pine nuts
- 1½ pounds ground lamb (not too lean)
- 2 tablespoons butter
- 3 cups long grain rice
- 3 cups chicken broth or stock
- ½ cup sliced almonds

1. Preheat oven to 350 degrees.

2. Combine chicken with water in a 9 by 13-inch baking pan. Hand rub salt and pepper over the chicken and bake for approximately 1½ hours or until cooked through.

3. Remove chicken from pan and strain the drippings into a medium mixing bowl. Set chicken and drippings aside to cool. After drippings are cool, cover and place in the refrigerator until the fat rises to the top. Skim off fat and set aside.

4. Heat 1 tablespoon oil in a large skillet over medium high heat. Reduce heat to medium, add the pine nuts, and stir briskly to avoid burning. Once pine nuts are brown, remove with a slotted spoon and set aside in a bowl.

5. Brown the ground lamb in the same skillet, being careful not to overcook. Season with salt and pepper to taste. Add pine nuts, mix together, and set aside.

6. After the chicken is cool, remove the chicken meat from the bones and cut into medium-sized pieces. Set aside.

7. Melt butter in a medium saucepan over medium high heat. Add long grain rice and salt and pepper to taste; stir until rice absorbs butter. Add approximately half the chicken drippings and chicken broth or stock. Bring to a boil

and then reduce heat to low. Cover and let simmer until the liquid is absorbed and the rice is fluffy when flaked with a fork.

8. Preheat oven to 350 degrees.

9. Cover the bottom of an ungreased 9 by 13-inch baking pan with ground lamb mixture. Add chicken, the rest of the chicken drippings, sliced almonds, and cooked rice; mix together and cover with aluminum foil. Bake for approximately 15 minutes or until all the broth is absorbed.

10. Remove from oven and allow to cool for a few minutes before serving.

Crab Stuffed Haddock with Sauce Creole

Recipe donated by Marc Chandler
SERVES 4 TO 6

- 2 pounds fresh whole haddock, fillet of sole, or Grey sole, cleaned
- 2 tablespoons olive oil
- Salt and pepper to taste
- 1 cup fresh crabmeat
- ¼ pound butter, melted
- 1 bunch fresh parsley, chopped
- 1 box Ritz crackers (3 sleeves), finely crushed
- 1 teaspoon Tabasco sauce

Sauce Creole:
- 2 tablespoons olive oil
- 1 stalk celery, chopped
- 1 red pepper, seeded and chopped
- 4 scallions, chopped
- 2 cups fresh tomatoes, peeled, seeded, and diced
- 2 tablespoons fresh parsley, chopped
- ½ teaspoon Tabasco sauce
- Salt and pepper to taste

1. Preheat oven to 350 degrees.

2. Wash fish inside and out under cold water; drain and pat dry with paper towels. Lightly brush the inside cavity of the fish with olive oil, salt, and pepper. Place fish in a greased 9 by 13-inch baking pan; set aside.

3. Combine crabmeat, melted butter, parsley, crushed Ritz crackers, and Tabasco sauce in a medium mixing bowl; mix until all ingredients are combined. Fill inside cavity of fish with stuffing and secure the opening with skewers or wooden picks. Brush the remaining olive oil on top of the fish.

4. Place pan with fish in the oven and bake for approximately 25 to 30 minutes or until fish flakes with a fork.

My father served this recipe, one of his favorites, in many Boston restaurants. He was known around town as "Chef Chandler" and cooked at many places including Tim's Tavern on Columbus Avenue and Chef Chandler's Commonwealth Grill, both in the South End. Sadly, my father passed away but his cooking lives on in the hearts of many.

5. Make sauce by heating oil in a medium saucepan over medium heat. Add celery, red pepper, and scallions. Sauté for approximately 5 to 10 minutes. Add tomatoes, parsley, Tabasco sauce, and salt and pepper to taste. Stir, reduce heat to low, and let simmer for approximately 20 minutes.

6. Remove fish from oven when done and transfer to a large serving plate or individual plates. Ladle sauce over fish.

Stewed Snapper Fish

Recipe donated by Hattie Frazier
SERVES 5

3	medium-sized snapper, halved
2½	limes
¾	cup oil
1	tablespoon salt or seasoned salt
½	tablespoon pepper
1	tablespoon paprika
1	medium onion, peeled and sliced
½	green or red bell pepper, seeded and sliced
1½	cups stewed tomatoes
½	cup water
1	teaspoon salt

1. Combine snapper with juice from 2 limes in a shallow pan or marinating bowl. Toss and marinate for approximately 15 minutes.

2. Heat oil in a large skillet over medium heat.

3. Remove fish from marinade and pat dry with paper towels. Reserve the marinade. Season both sides of fish with salt, pepper, and paprika, then place in the heated oil. Cook until both sides are brown. Remove fish from skillet and set aside. Discard all but about 2 tablespoons of the oil in the pan.

4. Add onion and pepper to the pan and sauté until medium soft. Add stewed tomatoes, water, 1 teaspoon salt, reserved marinade, and juice from remaining ½ lime; mix well.

5. Return fish to the skillet. Cover and stew over medium heat for 15 to 20 minutes. Serve warm with white rice or pigeon peas and rice and a side salad.

Hattie's Conch Fritters

Recipe donated by Michelle Carter

 MAKES 10 TO 15 FRITTERS

5–6 conch

½ cup vegetable oil

2 cups self-rising flour

½ tablespoon paprika

¼ teaspoon pepper

½ teaspoon salt

¼ cup tomato sauce

1½ cups cool water

1 medium onion, peeled and chopped

1 small pepper, green or red, seeded and chopped

When my mother, Hattie Frazier, was nine years old, she learned her family's secret recipe for Conch Fritters. She grew up in Miami, where her family was so well known around town for their fritters that people came to the house to purchase these tasty treats. Instead of a lemonade stand, my mother practically sold conch fritters door-to-door. Around the Christmas holiday, my mother sold them at the Mason Parade—10 cents for a small fritter, 25 cents for a medium fritter, and a dollar for a full-skillet fritter. She also sold them during the Steel Drum and Calypso Bands Annual Parades.

1. Beat each conch hard with a meat pounder until the tough side is well tenderized. Cut conch into small pieces.

2. Heat vegetable oil in a heavy, deep skillet over medium high heat.

3. Combine self-rising flour, paprika, pepper, and salt in a large mixing bowl; mix well. Add tomato sauce and water; stir until well blended. Add conch pieces, onion, and bell pepper; mix until all ingredients are combined.

4. Drop 2 to 3 tablespoons of conch batter into the hot oil in the skillet, being careful not to crowd fritters in the pan. Fry for approximately 3 to 4 minutes on each side or until cakes are golden brown.

5. Remove from pan and set aside to drain on paper towels. Season with salt and pepper and serve while hot.

Baked Catfish

Recipe donated by Sherry Ellis
SERVES 4 TO 6

1	pound catfish fillet
½	teaspoon pepper
1	teaspoon garlic powder
1	teaspoon onion powder
¾	cup finely crushed Ritz crackers
¼	pound butter, melted

1. Preheat oven to 375 degrees.

2. Wash and clean catfish fillet under cold running water. Pat dry with paper towels. Place catfish in a baking dish large enough to accommodate the fish in one layer. Sprinkle with pepper, garlic powder, and onion powder. Spread evenly with Ritz cracker crumbs and top with melted butter.

3. Bake for 5 to 20 minutes or until fish is flaky. Place fish under the broiler and broil for approximately 3 minutes or until crumbs are nicely browned.

4. Remove from oven and allow to cool for a few minutes before serving.

Baked Red Snapper

Recipe donated by Leo Romero

SERVES 8

- 1 cup milk
- 1 teaspoon oregano
- 2 pounds red snapper fillet, cut into 8 pieces
- ¼ cup olive oil
- 1 onion, peeled and sliced
- 4 tomatoes, chopped
- 2 cloves garlic, finely chopped
- 2 tablespoons capers
- ½ cup black olives, pitted
- ¼ cup dry white wine
- ¼ cup lemon juice
- 1 teaspoon salt
- 1 teaspoon cumin
- ¼ teaspoon pepper

Fresh cilantro and lemon wedges for garnish (optional)

1. Mix milk and oregano in a marinating dish or shallow container. Add pieces of snapper and coat with milk mixture. Refrigerate for one hour.

2. Heat oil in a large skillet over high heat. Add onion slices and cook until tender. Add tomatoes, garlic, capers, black olives, white wine, lemon juice, salt, cumin, and pepper. Reduce heat to low and simmer, uncovered, for 15 minutes or until sauce is thick.

3. Preheat oven to 350 degrees.

4. Remove snapper from refrigerator, drain, and pat dry with paper towels.

5. Place each fillet in the center of a 12-inch sheet of aluminum foil. Divide sauce evenly and pour over each fish piece. Fold foil tightly over fish and place packets in an ungreased baking pan or jelly roll pan.

6. Bake for approximately 15 to 20 minutes or until fish flakes easily with a fork. Serve hot with fresh cilantro and lemon wedges if desired.

Baked Fish in Sour Cream Sauce

Recipe donated by Faina Goldman
SERVES 4 TO 6

- 1 pound red potatoes
- 4 tablespoons flour
  Salt and pepper to taste
- 1 pound cod fillet
- 2 tablespoons vegetable oil
- 5 tablespoons butter
- 1 cup sliced mushrooms
- 2 hardboiled eggs, chopped
- 1 cup sour cream
- 1 cup shredded cheddar cheese

1. Parboil red potatoes by placing in a medium saucepan with water to cover. Bring to a boil and simmer for approximately 8 minutes. Drain and set aside to cool.

2. Combine 2 tablespoons flour and salt and pepper in a small, flat bowl. Cut cod into 4 to 6 even portions and coat all sides with flour mixture.

3. Heat vegetable oil in a medium sized skillet over medium high heat. Reduce heat to medium. Lightly fry cod on both sides. Remove cod from pan and place in an ungreased baking or 2-quart casserole dish.

4. Heat two tablespoons butter in the skillet. Slice cooled red potatoes and sauté until cooked.

5. Combine one tablespoon butter with mushrooms in a small skillet and sauté until cooked.

6. Preheat oven to 350 degrees.

7. Sprinkle chopped hardboiled eggs over the cod in the casserole dish. Spoon sautéed mushrooms over the eggs, then top with fried potato slices.

8. Heat sour cream in a medium skillet over medium high heat. Melt remaining 2 tablespoons butter and combine in a small bowl with 2 tablespoons flour. Add to sour cream when it is near the boiling point; whisk well. Pour sauce over fish and potatoes.

9. Top with shredded cheddar cheese, place in oven, and bake for 5 to 10 minutes or until cheese is melted.

10. Carefully remove cod from the dish and serve hot.

Cod Fish Cakes

Recipe donated by Thelma Callender-Burns

✥ SERVES 4

 2 tablespoons vegetable oil
 1 cup finely chopped onion
 1 cup flour
 1 teaspoon baking powder
 ½ teaspoon salt
 1 egg, lightly beaten
 1 tablespoon butter, melted
 ¾ cup milk
 2 tablespoons finely chopped shallots
 ½ pound cod or salt fish, cooked and flaked
 1 tablespoon finely chopped hot pepper

1. Heat oil in a heavy, deep skillet over medium heat. Add onion and sauté until just softened. Remove onion from pan and set aside, leaving oil in pan.

2. Sift together flour, baking powder, and salt in a medium mixing bowl. Make a well in the center and pour in the beaten egg, melted butter, and milk. Mix together lightly. Add softened onion, shallots, cod or salt fish, and hot pepper; stir well.

3. Drop 2 to 3 tablespoons of batter into hot oil in skillet, being careful not to crowd the fish cakes in the pan. Cook for approximately 3 to 4 minutes on each side or until cakes are golden brown.

4. Remove from pan and set aside to drain on paper towels. Serve while hot.

Chatham Cod with Almond and Tomato Sauce

Recipe donated by Rich Vellante
SERVES 4

½–¾ cup extra virgin olive oil
1 tablespoon chopped garlic
¼ teaspoon hot pepper flakes
1 Spanish onion, peeled and sliced
12 tomatoes, skinned and seeded
½ cup capers
½ cup chopped almonds
1 teaspoon thyme
½ cup chopped fresh basil
1 teaspoon sugar
   Salt and pepper to taste
1½ pounds fresh cod
   Olive oil for brushing

As executive chef of Legal Sea Foods, Rich Vellante tastes many great recipes. The Chatham Cod recipe has been in his family for many years, and is one of his personal favorites. The sauce may be made one day ahead and refrigerated overnight.

1. Heat ½ cup olive oil in a large saucepan and lightly brown garlic and hot pepper flakes. Add onion and soften for approximately 10 to 12 minutes over medium heat.

2. Once onion is soft, add tomatoes, capers, almonds, thyme, basil, and sugar. Simmer over low heat for 10 minutes. Add salt and pepper to taste. Remove sauce from heat and allow to cool.

3. Preheat oven to 375 degrees.

4. Rinse cod with plenty of cold water and pat dry. Place sauce in a casserole dish or rectangular baking pan large enough to hold cod without crowding it and place fish on top. Brush with olive oil. Season with salt and pepper to taste.

5. Bake for 15 to 20 minutes. Test fish in the middle to ensure it is fully cooked before serving.

Double Stuffed Flounder

Recipe donated by Joe D'Agostino
SERVES 6

Stuffing 1:

2	tablespoons butter
3	cloves garlic, chopped
1¼	cups sliced mushrooms
2	tablespoons fresh parsley, chopped
12	ounces fresh spinach
	Salt and black pepper to taste
⅛	teaspoon nutmeg
8	ounces Boursin cheese

Stuffing 2:

2	tablespoons butter
3	large shallots, chopped
½	pound fresh lump crabmeat
¼	cup dry breadcrumbs
¼	teaspoon cayenne pepper
	Salt and black pepper to taste
¼	teaspoon Old Bay seasoning
2	tablespoons fresh parsley, chopped
¼	cup dry white wine

6	large flounder fillets
6	toothpicks soaked in water
2	tablespoons butter, melted
¼	cup dry breadcrumbs

1. Make the first stuffing by heating 2 tablespoons butter in a medium skillet over medium high heat. Add garlic and sauté until brown. Lower heat to medium and add mushrooms and parsley. Cook for 15 minutes. Stir in fresh spinach and season with salt, pepper, and nutmeg. Blend in Boursin cheese and stir until mixture is well blended. Remove from heat and set aside.

2. Make the second stuffing by heating 2 tablespoons butter in a medium skillet over medium high heat. Add chopped shallots and sauté until soft. Lower heat to medium. Add fresh crabmeat and breadcrumbs and season with cayenne pepper, salt, black pepper, Old Bay seasoning, and chopped parsley. Stir and cook for 7 minutes. Add dry white wine and stir. Cook until wine is reduced. Remove from heat and set aside.

3. Preheat oven to 300 degrees.

4. Place the flounder fillets on a large work surface. Cover each fillet with the first stuffing. Top the first layer with the second stuffing. Roll each stuffed fillet inward and affix with a toothpick. Place the fillets in a 9 by 13-inch baking pan. Brush with melted butter and sprinkle with breadcrumbs.

5. Bake for 20 to 25 minutes, or until flounder is flaky.

Sides

Mama Deda's Chickpeas

Recipe donated by Marisa Oliveri
SERVES 4

- 2 cups canned chickpeas, or dried (soaked and precooked)
- 2 cups water
- 4 tablespoons olive oil
- 2 cloves garlic, finely chopped
- 1 tablespoon chopped fresh rosemary
- ¼ teaspoon salt
- ¼ teaspoon pepper
- 4 tablespoons pastina (tiny pasta)

1. Drain and rinse chickpeas.

2. Combine chickpeas and 2 cups water in a blender or food processor until creamy, but not too watery.

3. Place blended chickpeas, olive oil, garlic, rosemary, salt, and pepper in a medium saucepan. Heat over low heat for 10 minutes, stirring occasionally.

4. Add pastina. Cook for an additional 10 minutes or until pastina is tender. Serve while hot.

Nona's Cabbage

Recipe donated by Virginia J. Valenti

~ SERVES 4 TO 6

This simple and tasty recipe has been in our family well over 100 years. It makes a nice, complementary side dish to any meat, fish, or main course.

    1 head Savoy cabbage
    ¼ cup extra virgin olive oil
    2 tablespoons chopped garlic
    2 cups dry croutons
    6 Boston lettuce leaves for garnish

1. Remove core from cabbage and cut into one-inch pieces.

2. Place olive oil in a medium saucepan and heat over medium heat. Add garlic and sauté until golden brown. Stir in cabbage pieces.

3. Cover pan and reduce heat to low, stirring occasionally. When cabbage is limp, add croutons, stir, and remove from heat.

4. Serve on a plate garnished with crisp lettuce leaves.

Cabbage Salad

Recipe donated by Mary Salkaus
SERVES 6 TO 8

1 large green cabbage, finely shredded
1 white onion, finely chopped
½ teaspoon salt
½ teaspoon pepper
¾ cup mayonnaise

1. Combine cabbage, onion, salt, pepper, and mayonnaise in a large mixing bowl; mix well. Depending upon the size of the cabbage, add more mayonnaise, if needed.

2. Cover and refrigerate for at least one hour. Serve chilled.

Cabbage with Creamy Caraway Sauce

Recipe donated by Cynthia E. Blain
SERVES 4 TO 6

This recipe has been a favorite in our family for many years. Over the years, the amount of sauce has been increased so the extra can be used as a creamy gravy to accompany meat dishes. If you really like caraway seeds, you can increase the amount by 1 to 1½ teaspoons.

- 3 tablespoons butter
- 1 small cabbage, coarsely chopped
- 1½ teaspoons salt
- 2 cloves garlic, minced
- 1 teaspoon caraway seeds
- ¼ teaspoon white pepper
- 1 teaspoon sugar
- 1½ tablespoons cider vinegar
- ½ cup sour cream

1. Melt butter over medium heat in a large skillet. Add cabbage, salt, and garlic. Reduce heat to low. Stir well, cover tightly, and simmer for 10 minutes.

2. Remove cover from pan, add caraway seeds, white pepper, sugar, and cider vinegar; stir well.

3. Mix in sour cream. Heat thoroughly but do not bring to a boil. Remove from heat just as sauce is about to boil.

4. Serve hot with kielbasa, frankfurters, ham, or other pork dishes.

Sauerkraut Apple Relish

Recipe donated by Laverne Bansmer

SERVES 4 TO 6

This variation of sauerkraut may be served as a side dish or used on sandwiches, in salads, or with bratwurst or sausages. It is light and refreshing and a nice change from plain sauerkraut.

1	apple, cored, peeled, and shredded
1½	tablespoons lemon juice
1	pound sauerkraut, drained and rinsed
3	tablespoons olive oil
1	teaspoon sugar
¼	teaspoon salt
⅛	teaspoon black pepper

1. Sprinkle apple with ½ tablespoon lemon juice.

2. Combine shredded apple, sauerkraut, and olive oil in a medium mixing bowl; toss well and set aside.

3. Combine sugar and remaining lemon juice in a small cup or bowl. Mix well to achieve a perfect sweet and sour taste. Add additional lemon juice or sugar, if needed. Toss with sauerkraut and apple mixture.

4. Add salt and pepper and toss well. Cover and refrigerate for at least 2 hours.

5. Serve chilled as a side dish or at room temperature if adding to a sandwich, hot dog, or sausage.

Stir and Steam Cabbage Medley

Recipe donated by Sherry Ellis

SERVES 6 TO 8

- 1 cup water
- ¼ pound butter
- 4 tablespoons margarine
- 1 clove garlic, minced
- 1 teaspoon garlic powder
- 1 teaspoon onion powder
- ½ teaspoon black pepper
- 1 medium green cabbage, shredded
- 5 carrots, peeled and sliced diagonally
- 1 medium green pepper, seeded and cut into strips
- 1 large onion, peeled and sliced, core removed
- 1–2 white or gold potatoes, finely diced with skins left on

  Salt to taste

1. Combine water, butter, margarine, minced garlic, garlic powder, onion powder, and black pepper in a medium stockpot. Bring to a boil over medium high heat.

2. Reduce heat to medium and add cabbage, carrots, green pepper, and onion. Stir and cook until tender but still a bit crunchy. Add potatoes. Cover and cook for 10 minutes, or until potatoes are soft.

3. Add salt to taste and serve.

Sherry's Fried Apples

This is a nice side dish for pork, topping for pancakes, or dessert with ice cream or whipped cream. The butter and brown sugar give it a nice syrup.

Recipe donated by Sherry Ellis

☙ SERVES 6 TO 8

- 6 tablespoons butter
- 6–7 apples (any variety, half peeled, half unpeeled), cored and sliced
- 4 tablespoons margarine
- ½ cup brown sugar
- ½ cup white sugar
- 1½ teaspoons cinnamon
- 1 teaspoon vanilla
- ¼ teaspoon salt

1. Heat 2 tablespoons butter in a large skillet over medium heat. Add apple slices and stir. Add remaining 4 tablespoons butter, margarine, brown sugar, white sugar, cinnamon, vanilla, and salt; stir to blend all ingredients.

2. Cover and simmer for 5 minutes. Remove from heat and serve.

Jacob Wirth's Pancetta Braised Red Cabbage

Recipe donated by Phyllis Kaplowitz
~& SERVES 6

2	teaspoons olive oil
½	cup pancetta, cut into thin strips
1	small red cabbage, thinly sliced
3	tablespoons Calvados (apple flavored brandy)
1	cup apple cider
	Salt and pepper to taste

1. Heat olive oil in a large sauté pan over high heat. Lower heat to medium and add pancetta. Fry until pancetta releases its fat and is slightly crisp.

2. Add red cabbage, toss, and heat for 5 minutes over medium heat, or until cabbage is slightly wilted.

3. Mix in Calvados and cider. Cook for 15 minutes or until the liquid is reduced by half.

4. Season with salt and pepper to taste. Serve while hot.

Colcannon

Recipe donated by Ray Gardiner

🍂 SERVES 16

8 pounds potatoes, peeled, cut in chunks

1 teaspoon salt plus more to taste

1 white cabbage

1 head kale

¼ pound butter

1 white onion

Pepper to taste

This recipe provides plenty of leftovers. It works best with an equal balance of cabbage, kale, and mashed potatoes. The colcannon keeps fine refrigerated, but amounts may be reduced by half.

1. Combine potatoes, one teaspoon of salt, and enough water to cover in a medium stockpot. Bring to a boil over high heat and cook until tender, about 20 minutes. Drain well and mash. Set aside.

2. Remove and discard cores from cabbage and kale. Shred and set aside.

3. Heat butter in a large sauté pan over medium high heat. Reduce heat to medium and add shredded cabbage, kale, and onion. Stir often. Cook until cabbage and kale are limp.

4. When cabbage and kale are cooked, fold in the mashed potatoes and season generously with salt and pepper.

Lukshen Kugel

Recipe donated by Sandra Diner Wrubel

SERVES 8 TO 10

My mom usually made this as a side dish for Rosh Hashanah. You may also add approximately 1 cup dried, chopped apricots or raisins, if you wish. The cornflakes are always my favorite part of this dish, making it a little different from other kugels.

- 1 pound broad noodles, cooked and drained
- 3 eggs, lightly beaten
- 1 cup sugar
- 1½ cups milk
- ⅛ teaspoon cinnamon
- 2 cups cottage cheese
- ¼ pound cream cheese, cubed
- ¼ pound white American cheese, cubed
- 1 cup sour cream
- ¼ pound butter or margarine, sliced in ¼-inch pats
- 4 cups crushed cornflakes

1. Preheat oven to 350 degrees.

2. Combine cooked noodles and eggs in a large mixing bowl. Add sugar, milk, cinnamon, cottage cheese, cream cheese, white American cheese, sour cream, and half the butter; mix together gently.

3. Pour mixture into an ungreased 9 by 13-inch baking pan. Sprinkle with crushed cornflakes. Place the remaining butter pieces evenly over the top of the cornflakes.

4. Bake for 1½ hours. Remove from oven and allow to cool for approximately 5 to 10 minutes. Cut into individual squares to serve.

Boiled Greens

Recipe donated by Angela Parris
 SERVES 8

  3 pounds fresh young turnip, collard, or mustard greens or kale
1½ pounds salt pork, rind removed, diced into one-inch pieces
  1 cup coarsely chopped onions
1½ cups boiling water
  1 tablespoon sugar
  1 teaspoon salt
    Fresh ground pepper to taste

1. Wash both sides of the greens. Trim any bruised or blemished spots with a sharp knife and strip stems away from the leaves. Wash leaves again several times in cold running water to remove all traces of dirt or sand. Chop greens into large pieces and set aside.

2. Fry the salt pork in a large, heavy skillet or 5-quart Dutch oven over medium heat. Stir frequently until pieces are crisp and brown and all fat is rendered. Transfer to a bowl.

3. Add chopped onions to the skillet and sauté until soft. Add boiling water and bring to a boil over high heat. Add the greens, salt pork pieces, sugar, salt, and pepper.

4. Cover pot and simmer over low heat for approximately 45 minutes, or until greens are tender.

Collard Greens

Recipe donated by Francine Smythwick
SERVES 8 TO 10

- 2 smoked turkey wings, smoked neck bones, or ham hocks
- 3 pounds fresh collard greens
- 1 teaspoon salt
- 2 cloves garlic, finely chopped
- 1 onion, peeled and chopped
- 1 beef bouillon cube

1. Place turkey wings in a large saucepan with just enough water to cover. Bring to a boil over high heat. Reduce heat, cover, and simmer for 30 minutes.

2. Wash collard greens. Sprinkle with salt and rinse in cold water. Cut into small, bite-sized pieces.

3. Add garlic, onion, and beef bouillon to the saucepan. Add the collard greens and simmer over low heat for approximately 45 minutes, stirring occasionally from top to bottom. Cook until the greens are completely cooked and tender.

4. Remove turkey bones and cut up turkey meat. Add meat to collard greens before serving.

Lobster Boniato Mash

Boniato is a white sweet potato from South America. It can be found in most grocery or international food stores.

Recipe donated by Felino Samson

SERVES 4 TO 6

- 1 2½ pound lobster
- 2 tablespoons tomato paste
- 4 boniato sweet potatoes, peeled and quartered
- 2 tablespoons butter
- ¼ cup cream
- ¼ teaspoon grated orange zest

1. Fill a medium stockpot ¾ full with water. Bring to a boil over high heat. Add lobster and cook for approximately 15 minutes.

2. Remove lobster from water and set aside to cool. Reserve approximately 2 quarts of the cooking liquid. Once lobster is cool, remove the meat, chop, and set aside. Save shells and body.

3. Place lobster body and shells in a large saucepan with 2 quarts of the lobster cooking liquid and add tomato paste. Bring to a boil and reduce to approximately ¼ cup liquid, or "lobster essence."

4. Place quartered boniato in a medium saucepan with enough water to cover. Bring to a boil and cook until soft. Drain water. Add butter and cream and mash as you would mashed potatoes.

5. Stir in chopped lobster meat, orange zest, and lobster essence. Mix until smooth.

Gingered Baby Bok Choy

Recipe donated by Felino Samson
SERVES 4 TO 6

½ teaspoon salt
4 baby bok choy, split lengthwise
2 tablespoons extra virgin olive oil
1 teaspoon fresh grated ginger
Salt and pepper to taste

1. Fill a large saucepan approximately ¾ full with water. Add ½ teaspoon salt and bring to a boil over high heat. Add bok choy and blanch for approximately 1 minute.

2. Drain bok choy and place in a large skillet. Add olive oil and toss over medium high heat. Add ginger and salt and pepper to taste. Toss well and serve while hot.

Union Oyster House Boston Baked Beans

Recipe donated by Bill Coyne

SERVES 8

- 1 pound navy beans
- 3 ounces salt pork, without rind, diced into ¼-inch cubes
- ½ onion, finely chopped
- 1 pint tomato juice
- ¾ cup molasses
- 1 tablespoon dry mustard
- 1 tablespoon garlic powder
- 2 tablespoons brown sugar
- Salt and pepper to taste

1. Pick through dried beans and remove any pebbles or foreign objects. Soak beans in cold water to cover for at least 12 hours.

2. Heat salt pork in a large saucepan over medium heat until brown and fat is rendered. Add onion and sauté until tender.

3. Add tomato juice, molasses, dry mustard, garlic powder, brown sugar, and salt and pepper to taste; mix well.

4. Add beans. Cover and simmer for at least 2 to 3 hours, or until beans are tender and sauce is thick.

Durgin Park's Boston Baked Beans

Recipe donated by Albert Savage
☙ SERVES 8

- 2 pounds beans, any type (California pea beans preferred)
- 1 teaspoon baking soda
- 1 pound salt pork
- 1 medium onion, peeled
- 8 tablespoons sugar
- 2/3 cup molasses
- 2 teaspoons dry mustard
- 4 teaspoons salt
- 1/2 teaspoon black pepper
- 1 cup hot water

1. Pick through dried beans and remove any pebbles or foreign objects. Soak beans in cold water to cover overnight.

2. The next day, drain beans and place in a medium stockpot with cold water to cover; add baking soda. Parboil beans over high heat for 10 minutes. Drain in a strainer and rinse with cold water.

3. Preheat oven to 300 degrees.

4. Dice the salt pork rind into 1-inch cubes. Place half of the salt pork in a 2-quart bean pot and add the peeled onion. Add beans and top with remaining salt pork.

5. Combine sugar, molasses, dry mustard, salt, and black pepper in a medium-sized mixing bowl. Add hot water and mix until smooth. Pour mixture over the beans.

6. Bake for approximately 3 hours or until beans are tender. Checking regularly, adding additional water as needed, making sure beans are always moist but not flooded.

7. Once beans are tender, serve hot.

Rice and Pigeon Peas

Most of these ingredients may be found in a large grocery store. If not, they should be available at a Spanish market.

Recipe donated by Ralph Parenio

❧ SERVES 6

Sofrito:

- 2 tablespoons olive oil
- 1 medium onion, finely chopped
- 1 medium green pepper, finely chopped
- 3 tablespoons cilantro, roughly chopped
- 1 garlic clove, crushed

- 1 link chorizo sausage or ¼ pound cured ham or ½ pound boneless pork, cubed, fried and drained in advance
- 2 cups Carolina rice
- 3½ cups chicken broth
- 3 tablespoons tomato sauce
- ¾ cup alcaparrado, olives and capers
- 1 packet Sazon con Achiote Seasoning
- 1 packet Jamon Seasoning
    Salt and pepper to taste
- 1 can Grandules Verde, drained and rinsed

1. Make Sofrito by heating olive oil over medium high heat in a large cast iron pot with cover. Add onion, green pepper, cilantro, and garlic and cook until soft. Transfer ingredients to a strainer over a bowl and set aside.

2. Return drippings from Sofrito to pan and sauté meat over medium high heat until brown. Remove meat and set aside, leaving oil in the pan. Add rice to the pan and stir until rice is well oiled. Add broth, Sofrito, and meat, stirring to combine.

3. Add tomato sauce, olives and capers, Sazon con Achiote (to give the rice color), and Jamon seasoning. Bring to a light boil over high heat.

4. Reduce heat to medium low, cover tightly, and cook for 25 minutes or until rice is done. If rice kernels are still hard after 25 minutes, wet a paper towel, place over rice, and replace lid. Cook until rice softens.

5. Lift cover and mix rice with a fork. Add salt and pepper to taste. Sprinkle grandules on top of rice. Cover and cook for another 5 to 7 minutes.

6. Combine grandules with rice and adjust seasonings to taste. Remove from heat and let sit for 10 minutes before serving.

Stuffed Baby Eggplant

Recipe donated by Lydia Capano

SERVES 18 TO 20

Marinara sauce:

- ¾ cup olive oil
- 1 garlic clove, finely chopped
- 7 cups peeled, crushed tomatoes or 2 28-ounce cans
- 1 teaspoon fresh parsley, chopped
- 1 teaspoon salt
- 1 teaspoon pepper
- 1½ cups water

- 10 baby eggplants
- 2 eggs
- 7 cups freshly toasted breadcrumbs
- 1½ cups grated Romano cheese
- 1 tablespoon chopped, fresh parsley
   Salt and pepper to taste

Topping:

- ½ cup Romano cheese, grated
- ½ cup fresh basil, chopped (optional)

1. Make marinara sauce in advance by heating olive oil in a medium stockpot over medium high heat. Add garlic and sauté until brown. Add crushed tomatoes, parsley, salt, pepper, and water. Bring almost to a boil, lower heat to medium, and simmer for 45 minutes, stirring occasionally.

2. Wash the eggplants and cut in half lengthwise. Scoop out the eggplant meat, being careful not to damage the eggplant skins. Coarsely chop the eggplant meat then boil or steam until translucent. Set aside to cool.

3. Boil or steam the eggplant skins until tender. Set aside to cool.

4. Drain the eggplant meat and press out all excess water with paper towels.

This wonderful Italian recipe was passed on to me from my mother, Olga Capano, who received it from her mother, Carmella Ferrani. Like many wonderful Italian recipes, there is some time and work involved in the preparation, but the taste is well worth the effort. Some of the ingredients may be prepared a day in advance. Choose firm baby eggplants with full color and no bruises.

5. Combine eggplant meat, eggs, breadcrumbs, Romano cheese, parsley, salt and pepper to taste, and 2 cups marinara sauce in a large mixing bowl; mix well.

6. Preheat oven to 350 degrees.

7. Fill eggplant skins with the stuffing. Place stuffed eggplant halves, stuffing side up, in two 9 by 13-inch baking pans. Top with the remaining marinara sauce and sprinkle with Romano cheese and fresh basil, if desired.

8. Bake for 45 minutes and serve hot.

Lithuanian Kugeli

Recipe donated by Nancy A. Savilonis

SERVES 8

6–8 ounces thick-cut bacon, sliced in
    small cubes

3 eggs

1 12-ounce can evaporated milk

3 pounds potatoes, peeled, grated,
    and excess water squeezed out

1 cup ham, cubed

1 medium onion, peeled and
    finely grated

1 teaspoon salt

1 teaspoon pepper

1 tablespoon butter, melted

This wonderful recipe was passed on to me from my mother-in-law. She learned it from her mother who was originally from Lithuania. The family moved from Lithuania to Argentina, and in 1917 landed on Ellis Island, eventually settling in Brockton. This flavorful dish should be prepared as specified. The potatoes will look done after baking for approximately 1 hour, but be sure to leave it in the oven for a full 90 minutes. The original recipe calls for two teaspoons of salt, but we reduced it to 1 teaspoon.

1. Preheat oven to 350 degrees.

2. Fry bacon until crisp in a medium skillet over medium heat. Set aside and retain bacon fat.

3. Beat eggs and evaporated milk in a small mixing bowl. Set aside.

4. Combine bacon with fat, egg and evaporated milk mixture, grated potatoes, ham, onion, salt, and pepper in a large mixing bowl; mix well.

5. Pour potato mixture into a greased 9 by 13-inch baking pan; mixture should be at least two inches deep. Pour melted butter on top.

6. Cover with foil and bake for 30 minutes. Remove foil and bake for an additional hour. Kugeli should be medium to dark brown on the top, yet thick and heavy, similar to the texture of cheesecake.

7. Remove from oven and allow to cool for a few minutes before serving.

Potato Casserole

Recipe donated by Tonny Wong
SERVES 8

- 6 russet potatoes, peeled and shredded
- 4 cups water
- ½ teaspoon salt
- ½ teaspoon lemon juice
- ½ pound bacon
- 1 medium onion, peeled and finely chopped
- 1 5-ounce can evaporated milk
- 5 eggs, lightly beaten
- 1 tablespoon butter, sliced in pats
  Salt and pepper to taste

1. Place shredded potatoes in a large mixing bowl. Add water, ½ teaspoon salt, and lemon juice. Set aside to soak.

2. Fry the bacon in a skillet until crispy; crumble bacon and reserve fat.

3. Preheat oven to 425 degrees.

4. Drain the shredded potatoes well and place in a large mixing bowl. Add bacon, bacon fat, onion, evaporated milk, eggs, and butter; mix well. Season with salt and pepper to taste.

5. Pour mixture into an ungreased 9 by 13-inch baking pan. Bake for 30 to 45 minutes.

6. Cut into squares and serve hot.

Portuguese Stuffing

Recipe donated by Jon Bernier

- 2 linguiça sausages
- Giblets from turkey, chopped
- 1 tablespoon butter
- 1 large onion, peeled and chopped
- 1 loaf Portuguese bread, cut into large chunks
- ½ cup green olives
- 2 eggs, lightly beaten
- Salt and pepper to taste

1. Peel skin off linguiça and chop or grind up meat. Chop giblets. Set aside.

2. Heat butter in a large skillet or Dutch oven over medium heat. Add sausage meat, giblets, and onion. Cook, stirring, until sausage is cooked. Remove from heat and set aside.

3. Place Portuguese bread chunks in a large bowl. Add cold water to cover. Hand squeeze the bread to completely soak bread through.

4. Pick up a handful of bread and tightly squeeze out the water so it is damp, but not soggy. Place squeezed bread in pan with sausage and onion. Repeat until all bread is used.

5. Preheat oven to 350 degrees.

6. Rinse and drain olives. Chop and set aside.

7. Place pan over medium low heat and stir bread and sausage mixture to combine. Add eggs to stuffing and mix in well, being careful not to let eggs scramble. Add green olives and salt and pepper to taste. Pour stuffing into a 9 by 13-inch baking pan.

8. Bake for approximately 30 to 40 minutes, or until stuffing is crusty on top and warm throughout.

Hot German Potato Salad

Recipe donated by Virginia Korpal

SERVES 8

- 6 medium potatoes
- 6 slices bacon
- 2 tablespoons flour
- 2 tablespoons sugar
- 1½ teaspoons salt
- ½ teaspoon celery seed
- ¼ teaspoon black pepper
- ¾ cup water
- ⅓ cup vinegar
- ¾ cup chopped scallions, whites and greens

1. Boil potatoes in water to cover in a large saucepan for 25 minutes or until cooked yet still firm. Drain and allow potatoes to cool. Peel and slice potatoes with a sharp knife.

2. Fry bacon in a large skillet over medium heat. When almost crisp, remove from pan and set on paper towels to drain. Leave fat in pan. When bacon is cool, crumble into bite sized pieces and set aside.

3. Add flour to bacon fat and whisk over medium high heat. Reduce heat to low and continue to cook, stirring briskly, until sauce is smooth and bubbly. Remove from heat and stir in water and vinegar. Add sugar, salt, celery seed, and pepper. Test for sweet and tart balance; add additional sugar or vinegar if needed. Return to heat and bring to a boil over high heat for 1 minute.

4. Reduce heat to low. Carefully add potato slices, scallions, and crushed bacon. Stir until sauce coats all potato slices.

5. Remove from heat, cover, and let stand until ready to serve.

Rice and Peas

Recipe donated by Earlene Hardaway

SERVES 6

4 cups water

1 cup canned red peas or dry peas, soaked and precooked

1 smoked turkey wing

1 clove garlic, finely chopped

1 teaspoon thyme

½ teaspoon black pepper

1 teaspoon salt

2 scallions or leeks, chopped

1 tablespoon butter or margarine

1 onion, peeled and chopped

2 bay leaves

3 cups rice

1. Boil water in a medium stockpot over high heat. Reduce heat to medium and add peas, turkey wing, and garlic; simmer until peas are tender, but not too soft.

2. Add thyme, black pepper, salt, scallions or leeks, butter, onion, and bay leaves. Add rice and additional water, if needed.

3. Cook over medium heat, stirring once or twice with a fork, until rice is done, approximately 25 minutes.

Moroccan Fava Bean Salad

Recipe donated by Aziz Darouichi

SERVES 8

- 2 tablespoons extra virgin olive oil
- 2 pounds fresh fava beans
- 3 cups fresh chopped tomatoes
- 1 bunch fresh cilantro, finely chopped
- 1½ tablespoons lemon juice
- 2 teaspoons cumin
- 1 teaspoon coriander
- ½ teaspoon Moroccan harissa spice (found in gourmet stores) or red chili powder
- 2 cloves garlic, finely chopped
- 1 small white or yellow onion, finely chopped
   Salt and pepper to taste

This recipe works best using fresh fava beans. Fresh beans have a very tough skin. Avoid pods bulging with beans, which indicates that they are too old for consumption. Fresh pods should be blanched in boiling water for 3 minutes before being shelled. If using dried fava beans, soak for at least 36 to 48 hours in a large bowl with cold water. Boil for approximately 1 hour or until semi-tender, before using in the recipe.

1. Heat olive oil in a large saucepan over medium heat. Add fava beans, tomatoes, cilantro, lemon juice, cumin, coriander, harissa, garlic, and onion. Stir and cook for approximately 5 minutes, or until fava beans are tender. Remove from heat and set aside to cool.

2. Place in a large serving bowl. Add salt and pepper to taste, mixing well. For an extra spicy salad, add additional harissa spice.

3. Cover and refrigerate for at least 3 hours. Serve chilled or reheat over low heat for 15 minutes and serve warm.

Fried Cucumbers

Recipe donated by Esme Rajapakse

SERVES 4

1 large or 2 medium sized cucumbers
  Salt and pepper to taste
1 egg
1 tablespoon all purpose flour
½ cup dry breadcrumbs
½ teaspoon salt
¼ cup vegetable oil

1. Peel and cut cucumbers into quarters, then into 2 to 3-inch lengths; spoon out seeds. Generously sprinkle with salt and pepper and steam until tender.

2. Beat egg and pour into a shallow plate or bowl.

3. Mix flour, breadcrumbs, and ½ teaspoon salt in another shallow bowl.

4. Dip the cucumber slices in the egg first, then toss in the breadcrumb mixture. Make sure all sides of the cucumber slices are covered.

5. Heat 3 tablespoons vegetable oil in a large skillet over high heat. Lower heat to medium and fry cucumber slices until all sides are golden brown.

6. Remove cucumber slices from the skillet with a slotted spoon and drain on paper towels. Serve while hot.

Hush Puppies

Recipe donated by Beatrice Giggs

~ SERVES 4

2 cups cornmeal

½ cup flour

2 leveled teaspoons baking powder

2 tablespoons sugar

¼ teaspoon salt

1 egg, lightly beaten

1 onion, finely chopped

¾ cup milk

2 cups vegetable oil

Hush Puppies make an excellent accompaniment to chicken or seafood dishes. To vary this recipe, separate the egg and add yolk to the cornmeal mixture. Beat egg white until stiff and fold in.

1. Combine cornmeal, flour, baking powder, sugar, and salt in a large mixing bowl. Gradually add egg, onion, and milk; mix until smooth.

2. Heat vegetable oil in a large, deep skillet or stockpot over high heat. Oil is hot enough when a small amount of batter dropped into it rises quickly to the surface. When oil is ready, lower heat to medium.

3. Carefully drop 1 tablespoon of batter into the oil and fry until both sides are golden brown. Repeat until batter is used up.

4. Remove from the skillet with a slotted spoon and drain on absorbent brown paper or paper towels. Serve while hot.

Marinated Cabbage

Recipe donated by Mayya Yelyashkevich
🍃 SERVES 6 TO 8

This brilliantly colored side dish makes an impressive presentation. And it's extremely tasty, too! Makes a nice accompaniment to pork main courses, sandwiches, sausages, or potato latkes.

- 1 large green cabbage, shredded
- 2 carrots, peeled and shredded
- 1 medium beet, peeled and shredded
- 4 cloves garlic, finely chopped

Marinade:

- 1 tablespoon salt
- 1 tablespoon sugar
- 1 cup olive oil
- 1 cup vinegar

1. Place cabbage, carrots, and beet in a medium-sized stockpot. Add chopped garlic and set aside.

2. Make marinade by combining salt, sugar, olive oil, and vinegar in a medium bowl; mix well.

3. Pour marinade over vegetables in stockpot. Turn heat to medium high and bring to a boil. Once marinade begins to boil, immediately remove from heat and set aside to cool.

4. When cabbage is room temperature, cover and refrigerate for at least 3 hours. Serve chilled.

Marinated Cabbage

Recipe donated by Bella Karolinskaya
MAKES APPROXIMATELY 4 QUARTS

- 2 large green cabbages, about 2 pounds each
- 2 medium sized carrots
- 2 medium sized beets
- 4 cups water
- 1 cup vegetable oil
- 1 cup sugar
- 2 tablespoons salt
- 1½ cups vinegar
- 1 head garlic, cloves finely chopped

1. Remove cores from cabbages and cut into large pieces, approximately 2 to 3-inches each.

2. Peel and wash carrots and beets and cut into julienne strips.

3. Combine water, oil, sugar, and salt in a large stockpot. Bring to a boil over high heat. Add vinegar and remove from heat immediately. Do not allow the vinegar to boil. Cool mixture to room temperature.

4. Add cabbage, carrots, beets, and garlic to the marinade and gently mix. Cover and let sit at room temperature for 48 hours.

5. Place cabbage into individual sterilized jars and refrigerate for up to 6 or 7 days. Serve chilled or at room temperature.

Red Beans and Rice

Recipe donated by Irene Marsh
SERVES 4

3	cups yellow rice, cooked
2	cups canned red beans, or dried beans, soaked and precooked
1	medium yellow onion, chopped
¼	pound bacon, cut into ½-inch pieces
1	clove garlic, finely chopped
½	teaspoon thyme
⅛	teaspoon cayenne or red pepper
	Salt and pepper to taste

1. Cook rice according to instructions on package. Set aside to cool.

2. Rinse and drain beans. Set aside.

3. Place onion, bacon, garlic, thyme, and cayenne pepper in a large skillet. Cook, stirring constantly, over medium heat until bacon is done. Add rice and beans and mix well.

4. Cook over low heat for approximately 20 minutes. Season with salt and pepper to taste. Serve while hot.

Red Beans and Rice

Recipe donated by Ettle Andfield

SERVES 8

4	cups water
4¾	cups white rice
2	cups canned red beans, or dried beans, soaked and precooked
1½	cups coconut milk
4	cloves garlic, finely minced
1	teaspoon thyme

1. Bring water to a boil in a medium saucepan over high heat. Add rice, return to a boil, and stir. Cover and simmer over low heat for half the time specified on the rice package. Remove from heat, drain, and set aside.

2. Cook red beans until tender in the same saucepan . Add coconut milk, garlic, and thyme; mix well.

3. Add half-cooked rice to the beans, cover, and continue to cook over low heat until rice is tender.

Chelo with Tahdig

Recipe donated by Safta Malka Sedighi

 SERVES 6 TO 9

- 8 cups water
- 4 tablespoons salt
- 3 cups basmati (not Carolina) rice, washed thoroughly
- ¼ cup melted butter or olive oil
- ¼ teaspoon turmeric
- ¾ teaspoon salt

This recipe, translated, means steamed plain rice with a golden crust. It's originally from Iran. The stockpot used should be large enough so the rice is able to roll around freely as the water boils. The better the quality and appearance of the tahdig, the better your grade as a Persian cook!

1. Bring water to a rapid boil in a large stockpot. Add 4 tablespoons salt. Add washed rice to water and boil for 5 to 10 minutes, or until rice is no longer crunchy, but still firm. Stir occasionally to prevent rice grains from sticking together. Drain rice in a strainer and put into a large bowl.

2. Place 2 tablespoons melted butter or oil in the now-empty stockpot. Swirl in turmeric and lightly sprinkle salt evenly over the oil.

3. Drop rice into the stockpot, one spoonful at a time, making a mound in the center so the rice does not touch the sides of the pot.

4. Using the handle of a wooden spoon, make holes in the mound of rice down to the bottom of the pot. Drizzle the remaining 2 tablespoons melted butter or oil among the holes in the mound of rice. Cover the pot with a clean dishtowel and then with the pot's cover. Make sure it is tightly covered.

6. Cook for 20 minutes over medium heat, watching carefully to prevent tahdig from burning. Reduce the heat to low and cook for an additional 30 minutes.

7. Transfer cooked rice with a spoon to a serving bowl. Recover the stockpot and soak the bottom in cold water for approximately 5 minutes.

8. Carefully loosen the crust, or tahdig, from the bottom of the pot with two large forks and carefully invert it onto a separate serving plate, trying to keep it all in one piece.

Potato Croquettes

Recipe donated by Greg Oleszek
 SERVES 8

- 2 pounds potatoes, peeled and cut
- 1 teaspoon salt
- 2 tablespoons butter
- 5 tablespoons cream or milk
- 2 eggs, lightly beaten
- 1 tablespoon fresh chopped dill
- 1 tablespoon fresh chopped parsley
- 1 small onion, finely chopped
- ½ cup flour
- 1 egg, lightly beaten
- ½ cup dry breadcrumbs
   Salt and pepper
- 3 tablespoons butter, oil, or fat for frying

1. Combine potatoes, 1 teaspoon salt, and enough water to cover in a medium stockpot. Bring to a boil over high heat and cook until tender, about 20 minutes. Drain, add butter and cream or milk, and mash until smooth. Set aside to cool.

2. Add 2 lightly beaten eggs, dill, parsley, and chopped onion to cooled mashed potatoes; mix well. Form approximately 2 to 3 tablespoons of potato mixture into a croquette with your hands. Repeat until all potato mixture is used.

3. Place flour, 1 lightly beaten egg, and breadcrumbs in 3 separate shallow bowls. Roll each croquette in the flour, dip in beaten egg, and then coat with breadcrumbs. Sprinkle with salt and pepper to taste.

4. Heat butter, oil, or fat in a large, heavy skillet over medium high heat. Lower heat to medium and fry croquettes until golden brown.

5. Remove from pan and drain on paper towels. Serve while hot.

Stuffed Onions

Recipe donated by Ruth Austin

❧ SERVES 10

5	large onions, peeled
1½	teaspoons salt
3	tablespoons butter
½	cup chopped carrots, peas, or any leftover vegetables
2	tablespoons fresh chopped parsley
2	cups dry breadcrumbs
½	teaspoon pepper

1. Preheat oven to 350 degrees.

2. Cut onions in half crosswise. Place in a medium saucepan and add enough water to cover. Add ½ teaspoon salt and simmer over medium heat until almost tender.

3. Carefully drain onions, remove the onion centers without disturbing the outer layers, and finely chop the centers.

4. Heat butter in a small skillet over medium high heat. Add chopped vegetables and parsley; stir and cook until tender. When done, remove pan from heat and add breadcrumbs, chopped onion centers, 1 teaspoon salt, and pepper; mix well.

5. Carefully stuff onion shells with stuffing. Place stuffing-side up in a baking dish and bake for approximately 30 minutes.

6. Serve as a side dish with any pork or beef entrée.

Summer Squash and Zucchini Medley

In the past, vegetables were often prepared using a lot of butter. You may reduce the amount of butter and margarine used in this recipe by half.

Recipe donated by Sherry Ellis
SERVES 6 TO 8

- 4 tablespoons butter
- 3 yellow squash, cut in circles
- 3 zucchini, cut in circles
- 1 large onion, peeled and sliced
- 2 teaspoons garlic powder
- 2 teaspoons onion powder
- 4 tablespoons margarine
- 2½ tablespoons sugar
- ¼ teaspoon salt

1. Heat butter in a large skillet over medium heat. Add squash, zucchini, and onion; stir well.

2. Add garlic powder, onion powder, margarine, sugar, and salt; mix well. Cover and simmer until tender.

3. Drain excess liquid. Serve while hot with any meat dish.

Carrot Prune Stew

Recipe donated by Aronova Rakhil

    3 tablespoons butter
 1½ pounds fresh carrots, peeled and diced
    1 cup water
    6 tablespoons sugar
    1 pound dried pitted prunes
  ½ cup raisins
  ⅛ teaspoon cinnamon
    2 tablespoons orange peel
    2 tablespoons honey

1. Melt butter in a medium saucepan over medium high heat. Add carrots and stew for 5 to 7 minutes. Add water and sugar and bring to a boil. Reduce heat to low.

2. Add prunes, raisins, cinnamon, orange peel, and honey; mix well, cover, and simmer over low heat for 2 hours.

3. Check liquid in pot and add additional water, if needed. Stew uncovered for an additional 20 minutes. Serve while hot.

Carrots with Green Grapes

Recipe donated by Leo Romero

SERVES 6

- 8 medium carrots, peeled
- 1½ teaspoons salt
- 2 tablespoons butter
- 1 tablespoon sugar
- 2 cups seedless green grapes
- ¼ teaspoon tarragon
- ½ cup sour cream
- 2 tablespoons water

1. Cut carrots in half crosswise. Cut each half lengthwise into ½-inch strips. Fill a medium saucepan with 1 inch of water and ½ teaspoon salt. Bring to a boil over high heat. Add carrots, reduce heat, cover, and cook for 5 minutes or until carrots are tender but still crisp.

2. Melt butter in a medium skillet over medium high heat. Add carrots, sugar, and salt; stir and cook for 5 minutes. Add grapes and tarragon and cook until all ingredients are hot.

3. Remove from heat and stir in sour cream and water. Serve while hot.

Mashed Green Plantains

Recipe donated by Beulah Providence

SERVES 4

 2 green plantains, peeled and halved
 ½ cup milk
 5 tablespoons butter
    Salt and pepper to taste

1. Heat approximately 6 cups water to a boil in a medium saucepan over high heat. Add plantains to water and boil for approximately 45 minutes, or until plantains are soft.

2. Drain water from plantains. Add milk and butter. Work to a mashed potato texture with a potato masher or hand mixer.

3. Add salt and pepper to taste, and stir well. Serve with any meat dish as an alternative to mashed potatoes.

Mashed Potatoes and Carrots

Recipe donated by Mildred Shorr
~ SERVES 4

2	cups chicken broth
4	medium carrots, peeled and cut into ½-inch slices
2	medium potatoes, peeled and cut into 2-inch pieces
½	cup half and half
1	tablespoon butter
1	teaspoon cumin
1	teaspoon cinnamon
¼	teaspoon nutmeg

1. Heat chicken broth to boiling in a medium saucepan. Add carrots and potatoes and return to a boil. Cover and simmer over medium heat for 18 to 20 minutes, or until tender.

2. Drain then mash carrots and potatoes until smooth. Stir in half and half, butter, cumin, cinnamon, and nutmeg. Serve hot.

Steamed Italian Peas

You may use frozen packaged peas or, as odd as it sounds, use fresh peas and freeze them for at least 3 hours.

Recipe donated by Sal Scamardo
SERVES 4 TO 6

2	tablespoons olive oil
1	medium-sized yellow onion, peeled and finely chopped
1	clove garlic, finely chopped
2½	cups fresh frozen peas
½	teaspoon salt
½	teaspoon pepper

1. Combine olive oil and chopped onion in a medium saucepan. Sauté over medium heat until onion is translucent. Add garlic, frozen peas, salt, and pepper; stir to combine.

2. Cover tightly and cook over low heat for 20 to 25 minutes. Do not add any water. Serve while hot.

String Beans

Recipe donated by Beatrice Griggs
SERVES 6

⅓	cup olive oil
2	cloves garlic, minced
½	cup crushed tomatoes
½	pound fresh string beans, ends trimmed and snapped in half

1. Place olive oil and garlic in a medium saucepan and sauté over medium heat. Stir in tomatoes, add string beans, and mix well.

2. Cover and cook for 20 minutes over high heat, reduce heat to low, and cook for an additional 20 minutes. Serve hot.

Broccoli Fritte

Recipe donated by Marie DiStacio
SERVES 4 TO 6

1	large head broccoli, cut into spears with 1½ to 2-inch stems
4–6	slices stale bread
5	sprigs fresh parsley, stems removed
4	leaves fresh basil
½	cup grated Romano cheese
2	eggs
2	cups vegetable oil for frying

1. Parboil broccoli spears in a medium saucepan in water to cover. Drain well. (You may do this in advance.)

2. Combine 4 to 6 slices stale bread, parsley sprigs, and basil in food processor. Chop until coarse to make 1 cup of fresh breadcrumbs. Add up to ½ cup Romano cheese to taste. Place breadcrumbs in a shallow bowl and set aside.

3. Beat eggs and set aside in a shallow bowl.

4. Heat approximately ¾-inch to 1-inch vegetable oil in a large, deep skillet.

5. When oil is hot, dip broccoli spears into egg, coat with breadcrumbs, and place immediately in fry pan. Repeat until pan is full, being careful not to crowd spears. Turn once with forks when breadcrumbs are golden brown. Cook second side and remove to a paper towel–lined plate. Repeat with remaining spears.

6. Serve warm with grilled meats, hearty soups, and casseroles.

Artichoke Casserole

Recipe donated by Marie DiStacio
 SERVES 4 TO 6

16–20	canned artichoke hearts
	Juice of 1 lemon
4–6	slices stale bread
5	sprigs fresh parsley, stems removed
4	leaves fresh basil
½	cup grated Romano cheese
3	tablespoons olive oil

1. Drain, but do not rinse, canned artichokes in colander. Run a paring knife around the base where heart is exposed, cutting away all leaves. Remove choke from the center of heart by angling the paring knife into the middle and turning the heart in a complete circle. Scrape any remaining fibers with knife tip, if necessary.

2. Peel the backside of heart and snip stem. Stem is edible if peeled and cooked with hearts. Place hearts in a bowl of cold water mixed with 1½ tablespoons lemon juice, until all are prepared.

3. Place hearts in shallow skillet with 1 tablespoon lemon juice and enough water to cover, approximately 2 inches. Bring to a boil over medium high heat. Reduce heat and simmer hearts until tender, approximately 20 minutes. Test with knife for tenderness at thickest part. Drain well.

4. Preheat oven to 350 degrees.

5. Combine 4 to 6 slices of stale bread, parsley sprigs, and basil in food processor. Chop until coarse to make 1 cup fresh breadcrumbs. Add up to ½ cup Romano cheese to taste. Moisten breadcrumbs with 2 tablespoons of olive oil.

6. Coat a 9-inch square baking pan with remaining 1 tablespoon of olive oil. Arrange artichoke hearts in one layer in the pan. Distribute breadcrumb mixture over artichoke hearts.

7. Bake for 20 minutes, or until breadcrumbs are evenly golden brown. Serve while hot.

Malagada–Italian Stuffed Spinach

This quick Italian side dish is from Calabresse. You may substitute escarole for spinach. Serve as a side dish with any roasted meat or use as a bruschetta topping.

Recipe donated by Marie DiStacio

SERVES 4

1	pound fresh spinach
4–6	slices stale bread
5	sprigs fresh parsley, stems removed
4	leaves fresh basil
1	cup grated Romano cheese
2	cloves garlic
1½	tablespoons olive oil
	Salt and pepper to taste

1. Wash spinach and remove stems. Steam or boil spinach in a medium saucepan until tender. Drain and press out any excess liquid, if necessary.

2. Combine 4 to 6 slices stale bread, parsley sprigs, and basil in food processor. Chop until coarse to make 1 cup fresh breadcrumbs. Add up to 1 cup Romano cheese to taste; mix well.

3. Sauté garlic cloves in olive oil in a large skillet until brown. When garlic is tender, squeeze with a fork and sauté for another minute. Remove any excess pieces and discard.

4. Place spinach and homemade breadcrumbs into skillet with olive oil. Heat thoroughly, stirring constantly, for 3 to 4 minutes. Be careful not to overcook.

5. Taste for flavor and add salt and pepper, if needed. Serve hot.

Greek Spinach Pie

Recipe donated by Amy Salvo
SERVES 8 TO 10

- 4 10-ounce packages fresh or frozen spinach
- 2 tablespoons olive oil
- 1 bunch scallions, finely chopped
- 2 cups cottage cheese
- 1 cup crumbled feta cheese
- 5 eggs, lightly beaten
- 1 tablespoon farina
- 1/8 teaspoon pepper
- 1/2 pound butter, melted
- 1 package frozen phyllo dough, thawed overnight in refrigerator

1. Wash and clean the spinach. Boil then drain well. When cool, squeeze out all excess water.

2. Heat olive oil in a medium skillet over medium high heat. Add scallions and sauté. Set aside to cool.

3. Combine cottage cheese, feta cheese, and eggs in a medium mixing bowl; mix well. Stir in spinach, sautéed scallions, farina, and pepper.

4. Preheat oven to 350 degrees.

5. Brush a 9 by 13-inch baking pan with melted butter. Add one phyllo leaf and brush with butter. Repeat, layering phyllo and butter, for a total of 10 phyllo leaves. Spread spinach mixture over phyllo. Top with an additional 10 leaves, brushing each layer with melted butter. If phyllo hangs out over the pan, fold in.

6. Bake for approximately 30 minutes or until top is browned. Cut into squares and serve.

Kasha Varnishkas

Recipe donated by Marlene Arnold
SERVES 4

3	beef bouillon cubes
¼	cup boiling water
¼	pound butter or margarine, melted
½	pound bowtie pasta
½	package buckwheat groats
1	egg, beaten
1–2	tablespoons butter

1. Combine bouillon cubes and boiling water in a small bowl. Stir well and add melted butter or margarine.

2. Cook bowtie pasta according to directions on package.

3. Combine groats and beaten egg in a medium saucepan. Cook over medium heat, stirring until groats are coated. Add bouillon mixture. Cover and simmer until groats are soft and liquid is evaporated.

4. When pasta is done, drain well and toss with butter and groats.

Desserts

Egg Nog

Recipe donated by Dorsey B. Baron

SERVES 20

12 eggs, room temperature, separated
¼ teaspoon nutmeg
1 cup sugar
2 cups extra heavy cream
8 cups whole milk
4 cups dry sherry
1 cup dark rum
2 cups brandy
1 cup Curaçao

Egg Nog is a true New England Christmas tradition. The original recipe called for setting the mixture overnight in the "buttery," where the lower window sash should be left open two inches to allow the cold night air to enter. The crust may be decorated with colored sugars in artful forms. This is considered the crowing glory for the most creative holiday presentation.

1. Beat egg whites until stiff in a large mixing bowl. Set aside.

2. Place egg yolks and nutmeg in a large mixing bowl. Beat and slowly add sugar; mix until creamy. Set aside.

3. Whip heavy cream to soft peaks in a medium mixing bowl. Set aside.

4. Combine milk with egg yolk mixture in a large stockpot, punchbowl, or crock; stir with a wooden spoon. Slowly add sherry and stir. Add rum, brandy, and Curaçao, stirring to combine.

5. Gently fold in the beaten egg whites and whipped cream. Pour mixture into a serving bowl, cover, and refrigerate overnight.

6. A crust will have risen to the top by the next day. Sprinkle with colored sugars or additional nutmeg and ladle into individual cups to serve.

Pastry Pie Dough

Recipe donated by Susan Able
MAKES APPROXIMATELY TWO 9-INCH ROUND SHELLS

- ¼ pound butter, softened
- 2 cups pastry flour
- 1 egg yolk
- ¼ teaspoon salt (optional)
- 2 tablespoons sugar (optional)
- ⅛ teaspoon lemon rind (optional)

This is a universal pastry dough recipe. Use salt only if making a meat or poultry pie. If making a dessert pie, add the sugar and lemon rind for an added twist. The pastry dough may also be wrapped in plastic and will keep in the freezer for up to 3 months.

1. Work butter into flour with a pastry cutter. Add egg yolk and work with fingers until thoroughly blended.

2. Gather dough to form a smooth cake. Cover dough and refrigerate for at least two hours.

3. Roll the dough out thin for pastries or pies or use to line large pastry forms.

Mom's Clear Vanilla Sauce

Recipe donated by Kevin Swain
MAKES 3 CUPS

- 1 cup sugar
- 2 tablespoons cornstarch
- 2 cups water
- 3 tablespoons butter, melted
- 2 teaspoons vanilla

1. Combine sugar and cornstarch in a medium saucepan over medium-high heat. Slowly add water, stir, and bring to a boil. Boil for 1 minute, stirring constantly. Remove from heat and set aside.

2. Add butter and vanilla; whisk in briskly until sauce is smooth. Allow to cool. Serve on pound cake or plain cheesecake.

Molasses Cookies

Recipe donated by Hester Stanley Rundle

🍃 MAKES APPROXIMATELY 4 DOZEN COOKIES

Grandma Rundle lived independently until she reached the age of 93. She made these delicious molasses cookies for summer picnics at Seneca Lake in upstate New York.

- ¾ cup vegetable shortening
- 1 cup dark brown sugar
- 1 egg
- ¼ cup molasses
- 2¼ cups flour
- 2 teaspoons baking soda
- 1 teaspoon cinnamon
- ½ teaspoon ground cloves
- ¼ teaspoon salt
- ½ cup sugar for sprinkling

1. Preheat oven to 350 degrees.

2. Combine shortening, brown sugar, egg, and molasses in a large mixing bowl; cream with paddle or spoon until smooth.

3. Sift together flour, baking soda, cinnamon, ground cloves, and salt. Add to creamed mixture and mix until well blended. Cover the batter and chill in the refrigerator for one hour.

4. Line two cookie sheets with parchment paper. Using a tablespoon, drop batter on the cookie sheet. Lightly sprinkle the tops with sugar.

5. Bake for about 10 to 12 minutes. Remove from oven and allow to cool before serving.

Aunt Mame's Molasses Cookies

Recipe donated by Mary Shea Stratford

🐘 MAKES APPROXIMATELY 4 DOZEN COOKIES

½	pound butter, softened
1	cup sugar
1	cup molasses
1	cup sour milk
½	teaspoon ginger
1	teaspoon cinnamon
½	teaspoon salt
1	teaspoon baking soda
½	teaspoon nutmeg
2	eggs
5–6	cups flour

This recipe belonged to my great grandmother, and has been in our family for over 80 years. It's nice to use several different cookie cutters for a variety of shapes. If sour milk is unavailable, try this handy trick: combine 1 tablespoon lemon juice or white vinegar with enough milk to make one cup. Stir and let sit for 5 minutes before using.

1. Preheat oven to 375 degrees.

2. Combine butter with sugar in a large mixing bowl; cream until smooth.

3. Add molasses, sour milk, ginger, cinnamon, salt, baking soda, nutmeg, and eggs; mix until all ingredients are combined.

4. Gradually mix in 5 cups flour. Depending on the size of the eggs used, add more flour, if needed, to make a thick batter.

5. Roll the dough out on a clean work surface. Cut the dough with an assortment of cookie cutters and place on cookie sheets.

6. Bake for about 12 to 15 minutes. Remove from oven and allow to cool before serving.

Baklava

Recipe donated by Lorraine David Maloof
❧ SERVES 8 TO 10

- 6 cups sugar
- ½ lemon, juice only (approximately 1 ½ tablespoons)
- 3 teaspoons rose water
- 1 pound unsalted butter
- 2 pounds walnuts, coarsely ground
- 2 pounds phyllo dough, 1 pound for bottom layer, 1 pound for top layer (Greek baklava dough is best)

1. Mix 5 cups of sugar and 2½ cups of cold water in a large saucepan over high heat and bring to a boil. After the mixture boils for a few minutes, add the lemon juice, then add 1 teaspoon rose water. Continue boiling until the mixture just begins to thicken. Remove from heat and set aside to cool.

2. Melt butter over medium heat in a medium saucepan. Set aside.

3. Mix the walnuts with 1 cup sugar, 2 teaspoons rose water, and a few drops of cold water in a medium-sized bowl.

4. Brush the bottom of a 9 by 13-inch baking pan with melted butter. Place the first sheet of dough in the pan and brush with butter. Repeat for each sheet until the first pound of dough is used.

5. Preheat oven to 325 degrees.

6. Pour the walnut mixture evenly over the top layer of the dough in the pan. Start the layering process again with the second pound of dough, brushing the top of each layer with butter.

7. Cut in diamond shapes with a knife through the top layer of the baklava before baking.

8. Bake for one hour. Check regularly after one hour until the baklava is golden brown; do not overbake.

This popular Greek dessert is always made for special occasions. It is best to prepare all of the ingredients one day ahead and to lay everything out before starting the baking process. Have walnuts ground, pans ready, butter melted, and syrup prepared and chilled. As you use each sheet of dough, cover the remaining sheets with a damp dish towel to keep them moist. Baklava dough is extremely delicate and can tear easily. It must not dry out or get too wet.

9. Remove the pan from the oven and let it rest for a few minutes.

10. Pour the cooled sugar syrup over the baklava. Cover and let sit overnight.

Vermont Maple Syrup Pie

Recipe donated by Jean Poutre
MAKES 1 PIE

- 1 9-inch pie pastry (see page 235)
- 2 eggs
- 1 cup lightly packed brown sugar
- 2 tablespoons flour
- 1 cup maple syrup
- 2 tablespoons butter, melted
- ½ cup coarsely chopped walnuts
- 1 teaspoon vanilla
- ⅛ teaspoon salt

1. Preheat oven to 400 degrees.

2. Line the bottom of a 9-inch pie pan with pie pastry. Trim and flute edges, but do not prick.

3. Beat eggs lightly in a medium mixing bowl. Mix brown sugar with flour in a small bowl; add to the eggs and blend well. Stir in maple syrup, melted butter, walnuts, vanilla, and salt. Pour mixture into pie shell.

4. Bake for 35 to 40 minutes or until filling looks set. Remove from oven and cool before serving. May be served plain or topped with fresh whipped cream.

Caramel Date Pudding

Recipe donated by Ruth Austin

SERVES 4 TO 6

1¼ cups sugar

2 cups milk

2 tablespoons cornstarch

¼ teaspoon salt

2 egg yolks

1 cup chopped dates

½ cup chopped walnuts

1 cup apples, peeled, cored, and
   chopped into small pieces

This can be a bit tricky to make the first time. The dates, nuts, and apples need to be folded in just as the pudding begins to set. If not, the pudding will become watery.

1. Caramelize 1 cup sugar in a heavy bottomed saucepan over medium heat. Stir constantly until the sugar becomes dark brown and liquid in form, about 6 to 8 minutes. Turn heat off and let cool for 15 minutes, making sure liquid does not harden. Slowly stir in milk and blend well. If sugar begins to harden, heat slightly over low heat to melt and blend.

2. In a small mixing bowl, combine cornstarch, salt, and the remaining ¼ cup sugar; mix well. Add egg yolks and stir to combine. Whisk the cornstarch mixture into the liquid sugar mixture. Cook over low heat until thick, stirring often. Make sure the cornstarch is completely dissolved or the pudding will become lumpy. Remove from heat and allow pudding to cool but not completely set.

3. When pudding is cool, gently fold in dates, nuts, and apples. Allow to set for a few minutes. Serve with fresh whipped cream.

Homemade Vanilla Ice Cream

Recipe donated by Ray Gadiner

SERVES 8 TO 10

You may add just about anything to the basic vanilla ice cream recipe. Crushed and drained pineapple, pitted and sliced cherries, or chocolate chips are all possibilities. Simply fold them in at the end of step 3.

- 6 egg whites
- 1½ cups sugar
- 12 egg yolks
- 1 quart heavy cream
- 4 teaspoons vanilla
- 1 teaspoon cornstarch

1. Beat egg whites with ¾ cup sugar on high speed until soft peaks form; transfer to a large mixing bowl.

2. Beat egg yolks and remaining ¾ cup sugar on high speed until mixture is stiff; add to the bowl with the egg whites.

3. Whip heavy cream, vanilla, and cornstarch on medium speed until almost stiff. Add to the bowl with the egg whites and yolks; fold the whipped egg whites, yolks, and cream together until mixture has a mousse-like consistency.

4. Pour the ice cream mixture into one or two airtight containers. Cover containers tightly and place in the freezer for at least 6 hours before serving.

Mango Mousse

Recipe donated by Leo Romero

✎ SERVES 12

- 4 eggs
- 3 egg yolks
- ½ cup sugar
- 2 envelopes unflavored gelatin
- 3 ripe mangoes, peeled, pitted, and mashed
- ¼ cup brandy
- ¼ teaspoon almond extract
- 2 cups heavy whipping cream

Garnish:

- Fresh mango slices
- 1 cup sweetened whipped cream

The best way to peel a mango is to score the skin in fourths. With a sharp knife, slice peeled fruit lengthwise close to the pit. If you have trouble getting the mousse out of the mold, float it in a bath of warm water for a few minutes.

1. Combine eggs and egg yolks in a medium mixing bowl. Mix for about 5 minutes until thick and lemon colored.

2. Combine sugar and gelatin in a medium saucepan over medium heat. Add the beaten eggs, stir, and cook until the mixture begins to boil slightly, then remove from heat.

3. Stir in mashed mangoes, brandy, and almond extract. Refrigerate until mixture mounds slightly when dropped from a spoon.

4. Beat whipping cream until stiff in a large chilled mixing bowl. Fold into chilled mango mixture. Pour into an 8-cup mold and refrigerate until mousse is firm.

5. Unmold, garnish with fresh mango slices or fresh sweetened whipped cream, if desired, and serve.

Mama's Indian Pudding

Recipe donated by Priscilla Richardson

SERVES 6 TO 8

This is a very old New England recipe that has been in our family for at least three generations. The presentation can be spiced up with ice cream or fresh whipped cream. It looks best on the table when served in individual bowls.

3 cups whole milk

3 tablespoons yellow cornmeal

⅓ cup molasses

½ cup sugar

1 egg, beaten

¼ teaspoon ginger

¼ teaspoon cinnamon

1 tablespoon butter

1 cup whole milk, cold

1. Preheat oven to 300 degrees.

2. Scald 3 cups milk in a large saucepan over medium heat, then reduce heat to low.

3. Mix yellow cornmeal with molasses in a small bowl, then add to the scalded milk. Cook slowly, stirring constantly, until mixture is thick.

4. Add sugar, beaten egg, ginger, cinnamon, and butter; mix until smooth. Pour mixture into a buttered casserole dish and bake for 30 minutes. Stir in 1 cup cold milk and bake for an additional 2 hours.

5. Serve warm in individual bowls with fresh whipped cream or vanilla ice cream.

Maple Roasted Almond and Swiss Chocolate Soup

Recipe donated by Markus Ripperger

SERVES 8 TO 10

- 1 cup slivered almonds
- 1 teaspoon maple syrup
- 1 quart whole milk
- 2 teaspoons vanilla
- 10 egg yolks
- ½ cup sugar
- 1 cup heavy cream
- 1 cup finely chopped bittersweet chocolate
- 1 teaspoon amaretto
- 1 teaspoon crème de cacao
- 1 teaspoon kahlua

Pictured above: Hampshire House executive chef Markus Ripperger, owner Thomas Kershaw, and his mother, Florence. Mrs. Kershaw, who just turned 100 years old, now lives in Florida. She requests this dish, one of her favorite desserts, when she returns to Boston and the Hampshire House to visit her son.

1. Toast almonds in a large saucepan over medium-low heat until golden brown. Add maple syrup, milk, and vanilla and bring to a simmer.

2. Beat egg yolks and sugar in a small bowl.

3. Add the egg mixture to the saucepan and heat slowly until almost boiling. Continue to cook slowly until mixture coats a wooden spoon. Be careful not to let the mixture boil.

4. Remove soup from the heat. Stir in cream and chocolate. Stir in amaretto, crème de cacao, and kahlua; mix well. Serve with your favorite cookies, biscotti, or wafers for dipping.

Italian Wine Cookies

Recipe donated by Elizabeth Y. Saccocio
~ MAKES 5 DOZEN COOKIES

- 1 tablespoon anise seeds
- 1 tablespoon cinnamon
- 1 cup plus 1 tablespoon sugar
- 2 tablespoons baking powder
- 1 cup olive oil
- 1 cup red table wine
- 5 cups flour

1. Preheat oven to 350 degrees.

2. Combine anise seeds, cinnamon, and 1 tablespoon sugar in a small mixing bowl and set aside.

3. Combine 1 cup sugar, baking powder, olive oil, and red wine in a large mixing bowl. Mix in flour, ½ cup at a time, and continue adding until mixture forms a dough. Cover dough with a moist towel so it does not dry out.

4. Place a little oil on your hands and roll one teaspoon of dough into a small cigar shape. Form into a wreath with the two ends criss-crossed at the bottom. Dip the top of the criss-crossed ends generously in the anise mixture. Place cookies approximately one inch apart on an ungreased cookie sheet. Press the criss-crossed section of each cookie horizontally with the end of a fork to lightly flatten.

5. Bake for 20 minutes or until cookies are light brown. Cookies will harden and set when cooled.

Cranberry Nut Bread

Recipe donated by G. Eileen Gladu

~ SERVES 8

2	cups flour
1	cup sugar
1½	teaspoons baking powder
½	teaspoon baking soda
1	teaspoon salt
¼	cup vegetable shortening
1	egg
¾	cup orange juice
1	tablespoon grated orange rind
½	cup chopped walnuts
2	cups coarsely chopped cranberries

1. Preheat oven to 350 degrees.

2. Sift together flour, sugar, baking powder, baking soda, and salt in a large mixing bowl. Cut in shortening and mix until mixture resembles coarse cornmeal.

3. Beat egg in a small bowl; add orange juice and orange rind and mix well. Pour egg mixture all at once into flour mixture; stir just enough to dampen. Carefully fold in nuts and cranberries.

4. Spoon batter into a greased 9-inch loaf pan. Bake for approximately one hour or until crust is golden brown and a toothpick inserted into the middle comes out clean. Allow cake to cool before removing from pan.

Date Cake

Recipe donated by Sally Landowski
 ❧ SERVES 8 TO 10

½ pound pitted dates
1 cup warm water
½ teaspoon baking soda
1 tablespoon butter
1 cup sugar
1 egg
1½ cups flour, sifted
½ cup chopped walnuts

1. Combine dates, warm water, and baking soda in a small bowl. Mix and let sit until dates are soft.

2. Preheat oven to 325 degrees.

3. Combine butter, sugar, and egg in a medium mixing bowl; mix until creamy. Add sifted flour and date mixture; mix well. Add chopped walnuts.

4. Pour batter into a greased 9-inch loaf pan. Bake for 30 minutes. Remove from oven and cool before serving.

Rhubarb and Walnut Bread

Recipe donated by Jim Poutre

~ MAKES 2 LOAVES

If you don't have buttermilk, you can substitute either one cup plain yogurt or one cup of whole milk mixed with 1¾ teaspoons cream of tartar. If using milk mixture, allow to sit for 5 minutes before using.

1½ cups brown sugar
1 egg
1 teaspoon salt
1 teaspoon vanilla
⅔ cup vegetable oil
1 cup buttermilk
1 teaspoon baking soda
2½ cups flour
2 cups diced rhubarb
1 cup chopped walnuts

1. Preheat oven to 325 degrees.

2. Combine brown sugar and eggs in a large mixing bowl; mix until creamy. Add salt, vanilla, vegetable oil, buttermilk, baking soda, and flour; mix until smooth. Fold in diced rhubarb and chopped walnuts.

3. Lightly grease the inside bottoms and sides of two 9-inch loaf pans. Sprinkle flour into each pan and shake to completely cover the surface of each. Shake out all excess flour.

4. Divide batter evenly between the two pans. Bake for 1 hour. Remove from oven and set aside to cool.

5. Once cool, place a plate on top of the pan, turn over, and gently tap out loaf. Chill before serving.

Chocolate Marshmallow Dessert

Recipe donated by Wendy Hartje

~ SERVES 8

1	cup confectioners' sugar
½	cup butter, softened
3	eggs, separated
½	cup chocolate syrup
2½	cups small marshmallows
15	graham crackers, crushed
1	cup finely chopped walnuts

This recipe comes from my grandmother, Lila Mae Hartje of St. Thomas, North Dakota. She made this every Thanksgiving for about as long as I can remember. When she passed away, my mother carried on the tradition. This recipe is made from coast to coast since our large family is now spread across the country. Buy high quality organic or farm fresh eggs, since raw eggs are used.

1. Combine confectioners' sugar and butter in a medium mixing bowl; mix well. Add yolks, one at a time, mixing well after each. Add chocolate syrup and marshmallows; stir well.

2. Beat egg whites in a separate mixing bowl until stiff peaks form. Fold into the chocolate mixture; set aside.

3. Combine crushed graham cracker crumbs with chopped walnuts in a small mixing bowl. Place half the crumb mixture in an ungreased 9-inch square baking pan. Press down to make a firm crust. Add the chocolate mixture. Top with the remaining crumb and nut mixture.

4. Refrigerate for at least 24 hours before serving. Serve chilled with whipped cream or vanilla ice cream.

Orange Slice Cookies

Recipe donated by Priscilla Richardson

🍂 MAKES ABOUT 5 DOZEN COOKIES

1 cup vegetable shortening

1 cup brown sugar

1 cup white sugar

2 eggs

1 teaspoon vanilla

1 teaspoon milk

2 cups flour

1 cup shredded coconut

1 teaspoon baking soda

1 teaspoon baking powder

½ teaspoon salt

1 cup finely chopped walnuts (optional)

1 pound soft, candied orange slices

These cookies are my personal favorite. Have plenty of flour on hand, literally, when handling the candied orange slices. They are extremely sticky, and flouring your hands prevents the candied orange slices from sticking when cutting them into sections.

1. Preheat oven to 375 degrees.

2. Combine shortening, brown sugar, and sugar in a large mixing bowl; cream well. Add eggs, vanilla, milk, flour, coconut, baking soda, baking powder, and salt; mix well. Fold in chopped walnuts, if desired.

3. Cut candied orange slices in half on a floured cutting board. Cut each half section in thirds, then again in half so there are 12 pieces from each full slice.

4. Drop batter using a teaspoon onto an ungreased cookie sheet. Top each cookie with one piece of orange slice.

5. Bake for 12 to 15 minutes. Remove from cookie sheet to cool.

Demph Noodles

Recipe donated by Joyce Marcel
≈ SERVES 8 TO 10

  2 cups pitted prunes
  2 cups tart sour cherries, pitted
  2 cups fresh seasonal fruit (optional)
  ½ cup sugar
  4 cups water
1½ tablespoons lemon juice (optional)

Dumplings:
  3 cups flour
  1 teaspoon salt
  1 tablespoon baking powder
  ½ cup sugar
  7 tablespoons butter or vegetable shortening
  1 cup milk or buttermilk

1. Combine prunes, sour cherries, seasonal fruit if using, sugar, and water in a large saucepan; bring to a boil over high heat. Reduce heat and simmer for 15 minutes. Sweeten with additional sugar to taste; should be tart as well as sweet. Add additional lemon juice if needed for tartness. Remove from heat; set aside to cool to room temperature.

2. Preheat oven to 350 degrees.

3. Combine flour, salt, baking powder, and sugar in a large mixing bowl. Cut in the butter or shortening with two knives or your fingers until the mixture has a breadcrumb-like consistency. Add the milk or buttermilk and mix well until the dough clumps together.

4. Roll dough by tablespoonfuls in your hands to form small, firm balls. Drop balls into the cooled fruit mixture. When all the dough is rolled, gently stir, then ladle fruit syrup over the balls. Pour entire mixture into a 9 by 13-inch baking pan.

This delicious dish has nothing at all to do with noodles. It's a unique recipe my mother, Rose Kampler Kagan, learned from her grandmother, Frederika Kampler. The recipe came from Germany sometime before the turn of the last century. "Noodle" may come from the German word for dumplings, knodel. My mother and grandmother served this plain, but I prefer topping this wonderful dish with ice cream.

5. Bake for 35 minutes, or until dumplings are a light, golden brown color.

6. Serve warm, plain or with light cream, sour cream, or vanilla ice cream on top.

Applesauce Cake Deluxe

Recipe donated by Marilyn M. Barron

SERVES 8 TO 10

½ cup vegetable shortening

¾ teaspoon salt

½ teaspoon cinnamon

½ teaspoon cloves

½ teaspoon nutmeg

½ teaspoon allspice

2 tablespoons cocoa

1½ cups sugar

2 eggs

1½ teaspoons baking soda

2 cups flour

¾ cup fresh chopped dates

¾ cup raisins

1½ cups applesauce, unsweetened

¾ cup chopped walnuts (optional)

1. Preheat oven to 350 degrees.

2. Combine shortening, salt, cinnamon, cloves, nutmeg, allspice, and cocoa in a large mixing bowl. Mix well, add sugar, then add eggs, one at a time, beating until smooth.

3. In a separate bowl, sift together baking soda and flour three times.

4. Combine dates and raisins in a medium bowl; mix and set aside.

5. Mix approximately 3 tablespoons of the date and raisin mixture into the batter. Alternate adding sifted flour and applesauce, mixing well. Fold in remaining date and raisin mixture and walnuts, if desired.

6. Pour batter into a greased 9-inch tube pan or a 9 by 13-inch baking pan. Bake for approximately one hour or until a toothpick inserted into the middle comes out clean. Cool before serving.

Peach Cobbler

Recipe donated by Esme Littleton
SERVES 6

  6 tablespoons butter
  1 cup self-rising flour
  1 cup milk
  1 cup sugar
  2 cups ripe peaches, pitted, thinly sliced, skin on

1. Preheat oven to 350 degrees.

2. Melt butter in a quart-sized casserole or soufflé dish in the oven.

3. Combine flour, milk, and sugar in a medium mixing bowl; mix well. Fold peach slices into the batter.

4. Once butter is melted, remove pan from the oven. Pour batter quickly into the casserole dish. Return to the oven and bake for 35 to 40 minutes.

5. Allow to cool before serving. May be served plain or topped with fresh whipped cream or ice cream.

Cheese Pierogi

Recipe donated by Greg Oleszek

SERVES 8

Dough:

- 2 cups flour
- 1 teaspoon salt
- 2 tablespoons butter, softened
- 1 egg
- ½ cup warm water
- 4 tablespoons butter for frying

Filling:

- 2 cups ricotta cheese, cottage cheese, or baker's cheese
- ⅛ teaspoon salt
- 1 tablespoon sugar

Fruit Topping: (optional)

- 3 cups fresh blueberries, strawberries, and/or boysenberries
- ¼ cup sugar, or to taste
- 1 cup water
- ½ cup sour cream for topping

1. Make dough by sifting together flour and 1 teaspoon salt in a mixing bowl. Add butter, egg, and warm water; mix and knead until dough is smooth. Turn the dough out onto a floured work surface. Roll out very thin using a rolling pin.

2. Make filling by combining ricotta cheese, cottage cheese, or baker's cheese, ⅛ teaspoon salt, and 1 tablespoon sugar in a medium mixing bowl; mix well and set aside. For optional fruit topping, combine fresh berries, ¼ cup sugar, and 1 cup water in a medium saucepan. Simmer for approximately 30 minutes or until water is reduced. Set aside to cool.

3. With the rim of a saucer or 5-inch round cookie cutter, cut the dough into rounds. Place 1 to 1½ teaspoons of cheese filling into the middle of each dough round. Fold circles into half moons and seal outer edge tightly by pressing with fingers or the prong end of a fork.

This recipe comes from my grandmother. The most difficult aspect of making pierogi for the first time is keeping the filling in place while boiling or frying. This takes some time to master. The smaller the size of each pierogi, the more skilled the baker is considered by peers.

4. Heat 2 tablespoons butter in a large skillet over medium-high heat. Reduce heat, carefully add pierogi, and fry lightly on both sides. Once golden brown on each side, remove from pan and set aside. Add additional butter, as needed, until all pierogi are fried.

5. Serve warm, plain or with a large dollop of berry compote topped with a teaspoon of sour cream.

Chocolate Chip Meringue Brownie

Recipe donated by Ethel Smith
SERVES 10 TO 12

> 1 cup vegetable shortening
> ½ cup brown sugar
> ½ cup white sugar
> 2 egg yolks
> 3 teaspoons water
> 1 teaspoon vanilla
> 2 cups flour
> ¼ teaspoon salt
> ¼ teaspoon baking soda
> 1 teaspoon baking powder

Topping:
> 1 package chocolate chips
> ½ cup chopped walnuts
> 2 egg whites
> 1 cup brown sugar

1. Preheat oven to 375 degrees.

2. Combine shortening, brown sugar, white sugar, egg yolks, water, vanilla, flour, salt, baking soda, and baking powder in a large mixing bowl; mix by hand or with an electric mixer set on low.

3. Spread batter into an ungreased 9 by 13-inch baking pan. Sprinkle chocolate chips and walnuts evenly over batter. Beat egg whites and brown sugar until mixture forms stiff peaks. Carefully spread meringue over top of the brownie batter.

4. Bake for 25 minutes or until meringue is a light golden color.

5. Allow to cool and cut into squares before serving.

Swedish Brownies

These light and tasty brownies may be served plain or with fresh fruit and whipped cream.

Recipe donated by Edythe Mae David

SERVES 8

    2   eggs, lightly beaten
    1   cup sugar
 1¼   cups flour
    1   teaspoon almond extract
    ¼   pound butter, melted
    3   tablespoons sugar for sprinkling

1. Preheat oven to 350 degrees.

2. Combine eggs and sugar in a medium mixing bowl; mix until smooth. Gradually add flour, almond extract, and melted butter; mix well.

3. Pour batter into a greased 9-inch square baking pan. Bake for 25 to 30 minutes. Remove from oven and sprinkle with additional sugar.

4. Allow to cool before serving.

Passover Nut Cake

Recipe donated by Sandra Diner Wrubel
SERVES 10 TO 12

- 12 eggs, room temperature, separated
- 2 cups sugar
   Juice and grated rind of 1 lemon (approximately 3 tablespoons juice)
- 1 cup cake meal
- 4 tablespoons potato starch
- 1 cup chopped nuts

1. Preheat oven to 350 degrees.

2. Combine egg yolks and sugar in a large mixing bowl; mix well. Mix in lemon juice and grated lemon rind. Sift together cake meal and potato starch. Gradually add to egg yolk mixture. Mix until smooth.

3. Beat egg whites until stiff in a medium mixing bowl. Fold egg whites into batter, then fold in nuts.

4. Pour batter into an ungreased 10-inch springform pan. Bake for one hour. Remove cake from oven and invert onto a cake rack to cool. Remove from pan and serve.

Coconut Walnut Squares

Recipe donated by G. Eileen Gladu

ᦏ MAKES 16 SQUARES

- ¼ pound butter, softened
- ¼ cup light brown sugar
- 1 cup flour
- 2 eggs
- ½ teaspoon salt
- 3 teaspoons vanilla
- 1 cup dark brown sugar
- 1½ cups shredded coconut
- 1 cup chopped walnuts

Frosting:
- 5½ tablespoons butter, softened
- 3 cups confectioners' sugar
- 1½ teaspoons vanilla
- 2 tablespoons milk

1. Preheat oven to 350 degrees.

2. Combine ¼ pound butter and light brown sugar in a medium mixing bowl; mix until creamy. Add flour and mix with a fork. Drop dough into a greased 8-inch square baking pan. Spread and pat down to form an even crust. Bake for 20 minutes.

3. Combine eggs, salt, and 3 teaspoons vanilla in a medium mixing bowl; mix until smooth. Add dark brown sugar, coconut, and walnuts; mix well.

4. Remove crust from oven and top with coconut batter; spread evenly over crust. Return to oven and bake for 25 minutes. Remove and cool completely before frosting.

5. To make frosting, combine 5½ tablespoons butter, confectioners' sugar, 1½ teaspoons vanilla, and milk in a medium bowl. Beat well until frosting is smooth.

6. Frost cake and let set before serving. Cut into squares and serve.

Celia's Shtrudel

Recipe donated by Rona Lee Matisoffn
　 MAKES ABOUT 4 DOZEN SLICES

Dough:

- 2/3 cup vegetable oil
- 1/2 cup pineapple juice from 8 ounce can of crushed pineapple
- 2 large eggs
- 1/2 cup sugar
- 3–4 cups flour

Filling:

- 1/2 cup sugar
- 1 tablespoon cinnamon
- 1/2 cup ground yellow raisins
- 1/2 cup raspberry or mixed fruit jam
- 1 cup crushed canned pineapple, drained
- 1/4 cup vegetable oil for brushing
- 1/2 cup crushed walnuts (optional)

1. Make dough by combining 2/3 cup cooking oil, pineapple juice, eggs, sugar, and approximately 3 cups flour in a large mixing bowl. Mix together until dough is easy to handle. Add additional flour, if needed.

2. Make filling by combining sugar and cinnamon in a small dish. Mix and set aside. Combine ground raisins, jam, and crushed pineapple in a medium mixing bowl. Mix and set aside.

3. Separate dough into five sections. Roll out each section to form a strip approximately 10 by 6 inches. Brush each strip with oil. Sprinkle with cinnamon sugar mixture. Place a narrow row of filling along each strip and top with chopped walnuts, if desired.

4. Preheat oven to 350 degrees.

My mother invented this recipe. Friends and relatives always said there was nothing quite like my mother's shtrudel. This is how it was spelled on her original recipe notes. She often carried a few pieces in her pocketbook just in case she ran into a friend. It was a special treat many people still talk about.

5. Roll each strip, starting at the long end, to make long, skinny logs. Brush each log with oil and sprinkle with additional cinnamon sugar mixture. With a knife, make four to five slight diagonal slits along the top of each log. Be sure not to cut through to the bottom of the dough. Place 2 to 3 logs on an ungreased cookie sheet.

6. Bake for 30 minutes or until light brown in color. Remove from oven and cool for a few minutes. Place on cutting board and cool completely.

7. To serve, cut logs diagonally to the preferred size.

Maamool

Recipe donated by Lorraine David Maloof

❧ MAKES ABOUT 5 DOZEN

- 3 cups semolina
- 1 cup flour
- 1 cup sugar
- 1 cup butter, melted
- 1 cup milk

Nut mixture:

- 2 tablespoons rose water
- 1 pound coarsely ground walnuts
- 3 tablespoons sugar
- 1 cup confectioners' sugar for sprinkling

One interesting tidbit about this recipe and the following maamool recipe, which was donated by Alice Resha, is that both families settled in Boston in the 1920s on Hudson Street, which is now considered Chinatown. Although the cookies are similar, they epitomize the family tradition of changing a recipe just slightly for a unique taste. If the mixture is too wet, increase flour to 1½ cups for a thicker consistency. A Maamool mould is available at Middle Eastern grocery stores.

1. Combine semolina, ½ cup flour, and 1 cup sugar in a large mixing bowl; mix well. Add melted butter and alternately mix in the additional ½ cup flour and the milk. Mix until the dough is smooth and does not stick to your hands.

2. Mix rose water, ground walnuts, 3 tablespoons sugar, and a few drops of water in a medium mixing bowl to make the nut mixture; set aside.

3. Preheat oven to 300 degrees.

4. Using your hands, roll the dough mixture into individual balls about the size of golf balls. Holding a ball, hollow out a hole with your finger large enough to accommodate a spoonful of the walnut mixture. Stuff all of the balls this way and close the openings tightly so that the walnut mixture is completely covered.

5. Place each ball into the maamool mould and press down. When the mould is full, place a board on top, turn over, then bang the maamool carefully out onto the board.

6. Place maamool onto an ungreased cookie sheet, allowing some space between cookies. Bake for approximately 10 to 12 minutes or until all moisture is absorbed and the dough appears puffy. Do not let maamool brown. Remove from oven to cool.

7. Using a small sifter, sprinkle powdered sugar over the maamool while they are still on the cookie sheet. Allow maamool to cool and harden on the cookie sheet before serving.

Maamool

Recipe donated by Alice Resha
MAKES 5 DOZEN

1   pound butter

2   pounds cream of wheat

2   teaspoons ground mahleb (available in Greek or Middle Eastern markets)

1   cup hot milk

2   cups flour

2   tablespoons baking powder

1   teaspoon salt

1   cup sugar

Nut mixture:

2   pounds chopped walnuts

3   tablespoons sugar

1   tablespoon flower water

1. Melt butter over medium heat in a small saucepan. Pour the melted butter over the cream of wheat in a large mixing bowl. Add mahleb and hot milk; mix well. Cover and let sit overnight. If refrigerated, let sit at room temperature for 1 hour before using the next day.

2. The next day, add the flour, baking powder, salt, and 1 cup sugar. Knead by hand; set aside.

3. Preheat oven to 325 degrees.

4. Mix chopped walnuts, 3 tablespoons sugar, and flower water in a medium mixing bowl to make the nut mixture; set aside.

5. Using your hands, roll the dough mixture into individual balls about the size of golf balls. Holding a ball, hollow out a hole with your finger large enough to accommodate a spoonful of the walnut mixture. Stuff all of the balls this way and close the openings tightly so that the walnut mixture is completely covered.

6. Place each ball into the maamool mould and press down. When the mould is full, place a board on top, turn over, then bang the maamool out carefully onto the board.

7. Place maamool onto an ungreased baking sheet, allowing some space between cookies. Bake for approximately 10 minutes, or until maamool are a nice light golden color. Allow maamool to cool and harden on the baking sheet before serving.

Cocoa Cookies

Recipe donated by Virginia Korpal

❧ MAKES ABOUT 5 DOZEN COOKIES

- 2 cups flour
- 1/8 teaspoon salt
- 1/2 cup cocoa powder
- 1 1/4 cups butter, softened
- 2/3 cup sugar
- 1 teaspoon vanilla
- 2 cups finely chopped pecans
- 1 cup sugar for sprinkling

These cookies are very fragile, so be sure to take extra care when handling them once baked. Make sure the pecans are double chopped so there are no large chunks. These unique cookies are not overly sweet and taste best when served with tea or coffee.

1. Sift together flour, salt, and cocoa in a medium mixing bowl; set aside.

2. Combine butter and sugar in a large mixing bowl; mix until creamy. Add vanilla, then flour and cocoa mixture in small amounts; mix until smooth. Fold in pecans. Cover dough and refrigerate for at least 2 hours.

3. Preheat oven to 350 degrees.

4. Remove dough from refrigerator. Scoop teaspoonsful of dough and hand-roll into smooth, round balls. Place balls on an ungreased cookie sheet and bake for approximately 16 to 18 minutes.

5. Spread doubled sheets of paper towels in a cool, dry location. Remove cookies from oven and place onto paper towels to cool.

6. Place 1 cup sugar in a shallow bowl. When cookies are cool, roll in sugar until evenly coated.

Cheesecake

Recipe donated by Renee Parris Brown

~ SERVES 8

Graham Cracker Piecrust:
- 1 cup finely crushed graham crackers
- 2 tablespoons sugar
- 2 tablespoons butter, melted

Cheesecake:
- 2 8-ounce bricks cream cheese, softened
- 2 eggs, room temperature
- 2/3 cup sugar

Topping:
- 1 cup sour cream
- 1 teaspoon vanilla
- 1/4 cup sugar

I obtained this recipe in 1979 from Marlese Negaborn, who received it from her mother. Marlese was a refugee from the former Czechoslovakia where her parents were killed in a concentration camp. Marlese lived in St. Croix until she passed away in the 1980s. She made this cheesecake in her home and sold it to several restaurants in St. Croix.

1. Combine graham cracker crumbs, 2 tablespoons sugar, and butter in a medium mixing bowl; mix well. Add additional melted butter if needed. Press mixture by hand into a 9-inch pie pan, making sure to coat the sides and bottom evenly. Refrigerate for at least one hour.

2. Preheat oven to 350 degrees.

3. Combine cream cheese, eggs, and 2/3 cup sugar in a medium mixing bowl; mix until smooth. Pour mixture into the graham cracker piecrust.

4. Bake for one hour or until the top rises and is light brown. Remove from oven and cool for 20 minutes. Do not shut off the oven.

5. Combine sour cream, vanilla, and 1/4 cup sugar in a medium mixing bowl; mix well. When cheesecake is cool, spread topping evenly over the top. Return to oven and bake for an additional 15 minutes. Remove from oven and cool before serving.

New York Style Cheesecake

Recipe donated by Roberta Rice

SERVES 12

Dough:

- 1 cup flour, sifted
- ¼ cup sugar
- 1 teaspoon grated lemon peel
- ½ teaspoon vanilla
- 1 egg yolk, room temperature
- 4 tablespoons butter, softened

Filling:

- 5 8-ounce bricks cream cheese, softened
- 1¾ cups sugar
- 3 tablespoons flour
- 1½ teaspoons grated lemon peel
- 1½ teaspoons grated orange peel
- ¼ teaspoon vanilla
- 5 eggs, room temperature
- 2 egg yolks
- ¼ cup heavy cream

1. Combine sifted flour, ¼ cup sugar, 1 teaspoon lemon peel, and ½ teaspoon vanilla in a medium mixing bowl. Mix and make a well in the center. Add 1 egg yolk and butter. Using fingertips, mix until dough comes clean from the sides of the bowl. Form dough into a ball and wrap in wax paper. Refrigerate for one hour.

2. Preheat oven to 400 degrees.

3. Grease the sides and bottom of a 10-inch springform pan. Separate the side panel from the bottom of the pan.

4. After one hour, remove dough from the refrigerator. Separate approximately ⅓ of the dough. Roll this out on a work surface. Place and form onto the bottom of the springform pan. Trim off the edge. Bake the bottom for 8 to 10 minutes, or until golden brown. Remove from oven and set aside to cool.

5. Divide the rest of the dough into three equal parts. Roll each part into a strip 2½ inches wide by 10 inches long.

6. When the bottom, baked crust is cool, reconnect the sides of the springform pan. Fit the three dough strips to the side panels of the springform pan, joining the ends to line the inside completely. Trim dough so that it comes approximately three quarters of the way up the side of the pan. Refrigerate until ready to fill.

7. Increase oven temperature to 500 degrees. Combine cream cheese, 1¾ cups sugar, 3 tablespoons flour, 1½ teaspoons lemon peel, orange peel, and ¼ teaspoon vanilla in a large mixing bowl. Beat at high speed to blend all the ingredients.

8. Beat 5 eggs and 2 egg yolks, one at a time. Add cream and continue mixing until all ingredients are combined. Remove springform pan from the refrigerator and pour in the filling.

9. Bake at 500 degrees for 10 minutes. Reduce oven temperature to 250 degrees and continue baking for one hour. Remove cake from oven and cool on a wire rack. Cover and refrigerate for at least 3 hours, or overnight.

10. Release springform latch and remove sides of pan before serving.

Cane Drunk Cherries

Recipe donated by Inna Spitserev

🐦 SERVES 8

- 1½ cups dark cherries, pitted (fresh or frozen)
- 1 cup cognac or brandy

Dough:
- 3 eggs
- ¾ cup sugar
- 1 cup sweetened condensed milk
- 1 cup sour cream
- ½ cup flour
- ½ teaspoon baking soda
- ½ teaspoon vinegar

Cream filling:
- 1 cup sweetened condensed milk
- ½ pound butter, softened (2 sticks)
- ½ cup cocoa powder

1. Soak cherries in cognac or brandy in a covered bowl; refrigerate overnight.

2. Preheat oven to 350 degrees.

3. Combine eggs, sugar, 1 cup condensed milk, sour cream, and flour in a medium mixing bowl; mix well. Combine baking soda and vinegar in a small cup; slowly add to dough and mix well.

4. Pour batter into a greased, deep round baking or soufflé dish. Bake for one hour. Remove from oven and set aside to cool.

5. When cool, remove from pan and place on a flat work surface or board. With a long, sharp knife, carefully cut a one-inch layer off the top of the cake. Remove and set aside.

6. Cut a circle one inch in from the perimeter of the cake, being careful not to cut below one inch from the bottom. With a spoon, carefully scoop out the insides of the cake. Set aside the scooped out cake. The walls and bottom of the cake should be approximately one inch thick.

7. Combine 1 cup condensed milk, butter, and cocoa in a medium mixing bowl; mix until smooth. Drain the cherries. Carefully fold the cherries and the scooped-out cake pieces in with the cocoa mix. Carefully spoon this mixture into the cake wall structure. Gently replace the top layer of the cake.

8. Refrigerate the cake for approximately one hour. Decorate the top with sweet whipped cream or any favorite frosting or topping.

Fall Pear Cake

Recipe donated by Susan Able

SERVES 8 TO 10

   7 tablespoons butter, softened
 ½ cup plus 1 tablespoon sugar for sprinkling
 ¾ cup flour
   2 large eggs, room temperature
   1 teaspoon vanilla
 ⅛ teaspoon cinnamon
   2 tablespoons pear brandy
   3 ripe pears, peeled, cored, and thinly sliced, drizzled with lemon juice to prevent browning

1. Preheat oven to 325 degrees.

2. Lightly grease inside bottom and sides of a 10-inch springform pan with butter. Pour 1 tablespoon of sugar into the pan, and shake to cover surface completely. Discard excess sugar.

3. Combine ½ cup sugar and 7 tablespoons butter in a large mixing bowl; mix until creamy. Add flour, then eggs, one at a time. Mix well. Add vanilla, cinnamon, and 1 tablespoon pear brandy.

4. Arrange pear slices in an overlapping circle around the inside perimeter of the springform pan. Place remaining pear slices inside the circle. Sprinkle remaining 1 tablespoon pear brandy over pears.

5. Pour the batter over the pear slices; use a spatula to get all the batter from the mixing bowl. The batter will not completely cover the pears but will spread as it bakes.

6. Bake for approximately 45 minutes. Remove from the oven and cool on a rack for at least one hour. Serve plain or with ginger or vanilla ice cream.

Amish Sugar Cream Pie

Recipe donated by Joan Able

∽ SERVES 8

- 1 8-inch piecrust (see page 235)
- ¾ cup sugar
- ⅓ cup flour
- ¼ teaspoon salt
- ⅛ teaspoon nutmeg
- 1½ cups heavy whipping cream
- 2 tablespoons butter, softened
- 1 teaspoon vanilla

This recipe originally comes from an Amish family who lived near my hometown in Indiana. It's quick and easy and always a special treat. You can use a frozen piecrust, but it tastes much better if you make your own. If you use a frozen pie shell, be sure to let it thaw completely.

1. Line the bottom of an 8-inch pie pan with piecrust. Trim and flute the edges; set aside.

2. Preheat oven to 425 degrees.

3. Combine sugar, flour, salt, and nutmeg in a large mixing bowl; blend ingredients well. Heat whipping cream over medium heat in a medium saucepan. Stir constantly until it begins to simmer.

4. Add hot cream to the dry ingredients in the mixing bowl while stirring. Add butter, mixing until it is melted. Add vanilla and mix until filling is smooth, frothy, and creamy.

5. Place the pie pan with pastry on a baking sheet. Pour the filling into the crust and bake for 15 minutes. Reduce the oven temperature to 350 degrees and bake for another 15 minutes, until filling is firm but still wiggles.

6. Remove from oven and cool on a rack for at least one hour before serving.

Lazy Daisy Cake

Recipe donated by Sally Landowski

SERVES 12

2 eggs, room temperature
1 cup sugar
1 teaspoon vanilla
1 cup cake flour
1 teaspoon baking powder
¼ teaspoon salt
½ cup milk
2 tablespoons butter

Frosting:

¾ cup brown sugar
½ cup melted butter
¼ cup heavy cream
1 cup shredded coconut

1. Preheat oven to 350 degrees.

2. Combine eggs, sugar, and vanilla in a large mixing bowl; beat until thick. Sift together flour, baking powder, and salt, then add to egg mixture; beat until well mixed.

3. Bring milk and butter to a boil in a small saucepan; add to the cake batter and mix well.

4. Pour batter into an 8-inch square baking pan. Bake for 35 to 40 minutes or until a toothpick inserted into the middle comes out clean. Remove cake from oven and set aside.

5. Increase oven temperature to broil. Combine brown sugar, melted butter, cream, and coconut in a small mixing bowl; blend well. If frosting is a little dry, add an additional 2 tablespoons of cream. Frost cake evenly.

6. Return cake to oven and broil for approximately 2 minutes or until coconut is golden brown. Cool before serving.

Chocolate Cake

Recipe donated by Sally Landowski
SERVES 12

 2 cups flour
 2 cups sugar
 1 cup water
 ¼ pound butter or margarine, softened
 1½ ounces unsweetened chocolate squares
 2 eggs, room temperature
 ½ cup sour cream or buttermilk
 1 teaspoon baking soda
 ½ teaspoon salt
   Chocolate or buttercream frosting (optional)
   Chopped walnuts (optional)

1. Preheat oven to 350 degrees.

2. Combine flour and sugar in a large mixing bowl.

3. Combine water, butter or margarine, and chocolate squares in a medium saucepan. Bring to a boil, stirring constantly. Remove from heat and stir into mixing bowl with flour and sugar. Add eggs, sour cream or buttermilk, baking soda, and salt; mix well until smooth.

4. Pour batter into an 11 by 7-inch baking pan. Bake for 30 minutes or until toothpick inserted in center of cake comes out clean. Remove from oven to cool.

5. Serve plain or frosted with any chocolate or buttercream frosting. Top with chopped walnuts, if desired.

Mississippi Mud Cake

Recipe donated by Marilyn M. Barron

SERVES 8

- ½ pound butter, softened
- 2 cups sugar
- 4 eggs
- ¼ cup cocoa powder
- ¾ teaspoon salt
- 1½ cups flour
- 1 teaspoon vanilla
- ½ cup shredded coconut
- 1½ cups chopped pecans
- 1¼ cups miniature marshmallows

Frosting:
- ⅓ cup cocoa powder
- ¼ pound butter, softened
- ½ teaspoon vanilla
- ⅛ teaspoon salt
- ⅓ cup milk
- 2 cups confectioners' sugar

1. Preheat oven to 350 degrees.

2. Combine ½ pound butter and sugar in a large mixing bowl; mix until creamy. Add eggs one at a time, mixing between each one. Sift together ¼ cup cocoa powder, ¾ teaspoon salt, and flour. Add to egg mixture; mix well. Add 1 teaspoon vanilla, coconut, and pecans; mix until smooth.

3. Lightly grease the inside bottom and sides of a 9 by 13-inch baking pan with butter. Sprinkle 1 tablespoon flour into the pan and shake to completely cover the surface. Shake out all excess flour.

4. Pour batter into the pan. Bake for 30 to 35 minutes or until a toothpick inserted into the center comes out clean. Remove cake from oven and immediately top with miniature marshmallows. Once marshmallows begin to melt, gently spread evenly over the cake. Set aside to cool.

5. To make frosting, combine ⅓ cup cocoa powder, ¼ pound butter, ½ teaspoon vanilla, ⅛ teaspoon salt, milk, and confectioners' sugar in a medium mixing bowl; mix until smooth and creamy. Once cake is completely cool, after approximately one hour, top with frosting.

Mom's Old Fashioned Chocolate Cake

Recipe donated by Mitch Kaufman
SERVES 10

- ½ cup vegetable shortening
- 1 cup water
- 3 unsweetened chocolate squares
- 2¼ cups brown sugar, firmly packed
- 2 eggs, well beaten
- 1½ teaspoons baking soda
- ½ cup sour milk (or ½ tablespoon vinegar with enough milk added to make ½ cup)
- 2¼ cups flour
- ½ teaspoon salt
- 1 teaspoon vanilla

Frosting:

- 2 unsweetened chocolate squares
- 1 cup water
- 1 cup sugar
- 3 tablespoons cornstarch
- ½ teaspoon salt
- 1 tablespoon butter, softened
- 1 teaspoon vanilla

1. Heat shortening in a medium-sized saucepan over medium heat. Add 1 cup water and 3 unsweetened chocolate squares; stir until melted and well mixed. Remove from heat and set aside.

2. Combine baking soda and sour milk in a small cup; mix well.

3. Mix brown sugar into well-beaten eggs in a medium-sized mixing bowl. Mix until smooth.

4. Preheat oven to 350 degrees.

5. Sift together flour and ½ teaspoon salt. Alternate adding the sifted flour and salt, chocolate sauce, and baking soda/sour milk mixture to the egg mixture; mix well after each addition. Add 1 teaspoon vanilla and mix until well blended. Batter will be thin.

6. Cut two sheets of wax paper in rounds to fit into the bottom of two 9-inch cake pans. Insert the wax paper then divide batter evenly between the two pans. Bake for 30 minutes. Cakes are done when a toothpick inserted into the center comes out clean. Remove from oven and cool.

7. To make frosting, combine 2 unsweetened chocolate squares, 1 cup water, sugar, cornstarch, and ½ teaspoon salt in a medium saucepan. Stir over low heat until sauce becomes thick. Add butter and 1 teaspoon vanilla. Stir until smooth. Frosting will have a pudding-like consistency.

8. Once cakes are cool, carefully remove from the pans. Place the bottom layer on a serving plate. Frost and then place the second layer on top of the first. Finish frosting the top and sides.

Oatmeal Cake

Recipe donated by Sally Landowski
～ SERVES 12

    1 cup rolled oats
 1½ cups water, boiling
    1 cup sugar
    1 cup brown sugar
   ½ cup vegetable shortening
    2 eggs, room temperature
    1 teaspoon baking soda
    1 teaspoon salt
 1½ cups flour
   ½ cup cocoa powder
    1 teaspoon vanilla

Topping:
    6 tablespoons butter, melted
   ⅔ cup brown sugar
   ¼ cup heavy cream
   ½ teaspoon vanilla
    1 cup shredded coconut, toasted

1. Preheat oven to 350 degrees.

2. Mix oats with boiling water in a small bowl; set aside to cool.

3. Combine sugar, 1 cup brown sugar, and ½ cup shortening in a large mixing bowl; mix until smooth. Add eggs, baking soda, salt, flour, cocoa, and 1 teaspoon vanilla; beat well. Mix in cooled oats, folding together all the ingredients.

4. Pour batter into a greased 10-inch tube pan or 9 by 13-inch baking pan. Bake for 30 minutes.

5. To make the topping, combine melted butter, ⅔ cup brown sugar, heavy cream, ½ teaspoon vanilla, and coconut in a medium-sized mixing bowl.

6. When cake is done, remove from the oven. Increase oven temperature to broil. Spread topping over cake; return cake to the oven and broil for about 2 minutes. Cool before serving.

Apple Tart

Recipe donated by Cynthia E. Blain

SERVES 8

Crust:
- ¼ pound butter, softened
- ⅓ cup sugar
- ½ teaspoon vanilla
- 1 cup flour

Filling:
- 1 8-ounce brick cream cheese, softened
- ¼ cup sugar
- 1 large egg, slightly beaten
- ½ teaspoon vanilla

Topping:
- 4 cups apples, peeled, cored, and sliced
- ½ teaspoon cinnamon
- ⅓ cup sugar
- ½ cup almond slivers

My mother made this dessert when her lady friends came for luncheon at our home. She always made two so the rest of the family would be able to have some as well. Walnuts may be substituted for the almonds —either way, this tart tastes great.

1. Make crust by combining butter, ⅓ cup sugar, and ½ teaspoon vanilla in a medium mixing bowl; mix until smooth. Slowly mix in flour until mixture forms a soft dough. Press dough onto the bottom and 1½ inches up the sides of a 10-inch springform pan.

2. Preheat oven to 450 degrees.

3. Make the filling by combining cream cheese and ¼ cup sugar in a medium mixing bowl; mix until smooth. Add egg and ½ teaspoon vanilla; blend until smooth. Pour mixture over crust in the springform pan.

4. Toss apples, cinnamon, and ⅓ cup sugar in a medium mixing bowl. Layer apple slices evenly over the cream cheese mixture; sprinkle with almond slivers.

5. Bake for 10 minutes, then lower the oven temperature to 400 degrees and bake for an additional 25 minutes. Remove tart from the oven and let cool completely before removing sides of pan. Serve at room temperature or slightly chilled with whipped cream or vanilla ice cream.

Apple Dumplings

Recipe donated by Miriam Robinson
SERVES 6

 2 cups flour
 2 teaspoons baking powder
 1 teaspoon salt
 ½ cup vegetable shortening
 ½ cup milk
 1½ tablespoons cinnamon
 1½ tablespoons nutmeg
 1½ tablespoons sugar
 6 whole Granny Smith or Cortland apples, peeled and cored
 2 tablespoons butter

Sauce:
 1 cup sugar plus more for sprinkling on top
 1 cup water
 ⅛ teaspoon cinnamon
 2 drops red food coloring
 2 tablespoons butter or margarine

1. Sift together flour, baking powder, and salt in a large mixing bowl. Cut in shortening. Add milk and stir until moist. Roll out dough on a lightly floured work surface until it is approximately 12 by 18 inches and ¼ inch thick. Cut dough into 6-inch squares with a sharp wet knife.

2. Combine 1½ tablespoons cinnamon, nutmeg, and 1½ tablespoons sugar in a small cup; mix and set aside.

3. Place one apple in the middle of each 6-inch pastry square. Sprinkle each apple top and inside each pastry square with the cinnamon, nutmeg, and sugar mixture. Dot each apple with 1 teaspoon butter, making sure all sides of each apple is covered.

4. Preheat oven to 375 degrees.

5. Moisten edges of each pastry square, wrap the corners toward the top center of the apple, and pinch the dough together with your fingers to hold it firmly in place.

6. Place apple dumplings into a greased 7 by 11-inch baking pan and set aside.

7. Combine 1 cup sugar, water, ⅛ teaspoon cinnamon, and red food coloring in a medium saucepan. Bring to a boil. Add 2 tablespoons butter and stir well. Once butter is melted, pour sauce over dumplings and sprinkle with additional sugar.

8. Bake for 45 minutes. Baste twice while baking. Serve hot with fresh whipped cream or vanilla ice cream.

Apple Crisp

Recipe donated by Flora Shattuck
~ SERVES 6

- ¾ cup brown sugar
- ⅓ cup butter, softened
- ½ cup flour, sifted
- 1 cup rolled oats
- ¾ teaspoon cinnamon
- ¾ teaspoon nutmeg
- 2 apples, peeled, cored, and thinly sliced

1. Preheat oven to 350 degrees.

2. Combine brown sugar, butter, flour, oats, cinnamon, and nutmeg in a large mixing bowl; mix well.

3. Layer apples into the bottom of a greased 8-inch square baking pan; spread brown sugar mixture evenly over the apple slices.

4. Bake for 35 minutes. Remove from oven and cool for a few minutes before serving. May be served plain or with fresh whipped cream or ice cream.

Greek Easter Orthodox Cookies

This traditional Greek Easter Orthodox cookie recipe has been in our family for well over 100 years. It was passed down to me from my grandmother who was born in Larissa, Greece.

Recipe donated by Susan Bamvakas

❧ MAKES ABOUT 9 DOZEN

½	pound butter, softened
2	cups sugar
7	large eggs, room temperature, lightly beaten
9½	cups flour
5	tablespoons baking powder
1	teaspoon salt
½	cup milk
1	tablespoon vanilla
1½	cups sesame seeds

1. Preheat oven to 350 degrees.

2. Combine butter and sugar in a large mixing bowl; mix until creamy. Add eggs and mix well.

3. Sift together flour, baking powder, and salt. Alternate adding flour mixture, milk, and vanilla to batter; mix well after each addition.

4. Place sesame seeds in a shallow bowl and set aside.

5. Place dough on a clean work surface and hand-knead well. Scoop 1 tablespoon of dough and roll by hand into a ball. Repeat until all dough is used. Dip tops of balls into sesame seeds, then place on a greased cookie sheet.

6. Bake for 15 to 20 minutes.

Vienna Torte

Recipe donated by Virginia Korpal
~ SERVES 10 TO 12

Cake:

     6 eggs, room temperature, separated
 1½ cups sugar
 ½ teaspoon salt
 ½ cup hot water
 1½ cups flour, sifted
 ½ teaspoon vanilla

Filling and frosting:

     3 cups whole milk
 ⅔ cup cornstarch
 ⅔ cup sugar
     2 eggs, room temperature
 ½ teaspoon vanilla
 ¾ pound butter, softened
     2 cups confectioners' sugar
     2 teaspoons cocoa powder
 ⅓ cup chopped walnuts (optional)

1. Preheat oven to 350 degrees.

2. Combine 6 egg whites and ½ cup sugar in a medium mixing bowl; beat until stiff. Set aside.

3. Combine 6 egg yolks, ½ teaspoon salt, and hot water in a separate, large mixing bowl; mix until thick and lemon-colored. Slowly add 1 cup sugar and mix until smooth. Continue mixing while slowly adding 1½ cups sifted flour and ½ teaspoon vanilla; mix until smooth.

4. Gently fold egg whites into the egg yolk mixture with a spatula. Mix until fully incorporated. Pour batter into an ungreased angel food pan. Bake for 45 minutes or until the top is golden and springs back quickly when pressed with your finger. Remove cake from oven and cool in the pan on a wire rack for approximately one hour.

5. Combine milk, cornstarch, sugar, eggs, and vanilla in a medium saucepan over medium heat. Whisk until mixture becomes thick and custard-like. Remove from heat and cool for approximately one hour.

6. Combine butter and confectioners' sugar in a medium mixing bowl; mix until smooth and creamy. Fold in cooled custard mixture and beat until creamy. If the custard is somewhat lumpy beat on high speed. Set aside.

7. When cake is cool, gently remove from pan and place on cutting board. With a long, thin knife, gently cut the cake horizontally into three even layers. Set the bottom layer on a large cake plate and spread the top only with approximately ¼ inch of the custard filling. Place the second cake layer on top and spread with another layer of custard filling. Top with the third cake layer.

8. Add cocoa to the remaining custard filling and mix until smooth. Frost the top and sides of the cake. Sprinkle with chopped walnuts, if desired.

9. Chill and remove from refrigerator one hour before serving.

Sunshine Cake

Recipe donated by Virginia Korpal

SERVES 8

Middle layer:

- 5 egg whites, room temperature
- 1 teaspoon cream of tartar
- ¾ cup sugar
- ½ cup flour, sifted twice
- 1 teaspoon vanilla
- ¼ teaspoon salt

Bottom and top layers:

- 5 egg yolks, room temperature
- 1 teaspoon cream of tartar
- 1 cup sugar
- 1½ cups flour, sifted twice
- ½ cup milk
- ½ teaspoon baking soda
- ¼ teaspoon salt
- 1 teaspoon vanilla

Boiled icing:

- 4 egg whites, room temperature
- ½ teaspoon cream of tartar
- ⅛ teaspoon salt
- 1½ cups sugar
- ½ cup water

1. Preheat oven to 325 degrees.

2. Lightly grease the inside bottom and sides of three 9-inch round baking pans with butter. Pour flour into each pan and shake to completely cover the surface. Shake out all excess flour.

3. For the middle layer, combine 5 egg whites and 1 teaspoon cream of tartar in a medium mixing bowl. Mix on high speed until approximately half stiff. Add ¾ cup sugar, ½ cup twice-sifted flour, 1 teaspoon vanilla, and ¼ teaspoon salt; mix well. Pour batter into one pan. Bake for 15 to 18 minutes.

4. For the bottom and top layers, combine 5 egg yolks, 1 teaspoon cream of tartar, and 1 cup sugar in a medium mixing bowl. Mix until almost stiff. Gradually add 1½ cups twice-sifted flour, milk, baking soda, ¼ teaspoon salt, and 1 teaspoon vanilla; mix well. Divide batter evenly between 2 pans. Batter will be light, but will spread as it bakes. Bake for 15 to 18 minutes or until a toothpick inserted in the middle comes out clean.

5. Cool the three layers in the pans.

6. For the icing, combine 4 egg whites, ½ teaspoon cream of tartar, and ⅛ teaspoon salt in a medium mixing bowl; mix on high speed until stiff.

7. While mixing eggs whites, combine 1½ cups sugar and water in a small saucepan; cook over medium-high heat until sugar is dissolved, stirring constantly. Bring to a boil and cover tightly. Let boil rapidly without stirring for approximately 5 minutes.

8. Once egg whites have stiff peaks, reduce speed to medium and slowly drizzle in hot sugar sauce. Once all sugar sauce is added, increase speed to high and mix until the meringue forms stiff and shiny peaks.

9. Place bottom cake layer on a serving plate. Frost with meringue. Place middle layer on top, press down slightly, and frost with meringue. Repeat for the third layer and finish frosting top and sides.

10. Cover and refrigerate. Remove from refrigerator approximately one hour before serving.

Buttermilk Scones

Recipe donated by Renee Covalucci

MAKES ABOUT 1 1/2 TO 2 DOZEN

This very healthy scone recipe comes directly from Italy from my grandmother, Giovanna Covalucci. Grandma Covalucci, along with her brothers, were all inventive and creative in the kitchen. This recipe is versatile, quick, and easy. You can mix and match any optional ingredients to your liking. My favorite is made with dried peaches, toasted sugared pecans, and raisins or craisins.

Dough:

4	cups flour
1/2	cup sugar
3	teaspoons baking powder
1/2	teaspoon salt
1/2	cup butter or margarine, softened
1/2	cup buttermilk
1	egg
1	egg white

Optional fillings:

1 1/2	cups dried fruit, chocolate chips, raisins, craisins, dried peaches, or toasted nuts
1	egg white, beaten
1/4	cup sugar
1	cup fruit preserves

1. Combine flour, sugar, baking powder, and salt in a large mixing bowl. Cut in butter or margarine until mixture is course.

2. Combine buttermilk, egg, and egg white in a medium mixing bowl; mix well. Add to the dry ingredients and mix by hand. Be careful not to overmix. Add optional filling ingredients, if desired.

3. Place dough on a flat work surface and knead. Turn dough over three times to incorporate any added dried fruit, chocolate chips, raisins, craisins, dried peaches, or toasted nuts. Turn dough over four to five times for plain or fruit preserve topped scones. Add little to no flour to board when kneading.

4. Preheat oven to 400 degrees.

5. Cut dough into four even pieces. Pat each section into a 1½-inch thick circle. Using a 3-inch drinking glass or cookie cutter, cut each section of dough into rounds. There should be approximately 6 rounds per section. Transfer rounds to baking pan or cookie sheet.

6. Optional fillings: brush with a beaten egg white and sprinkle with sugar. If topping with fruit preserves, gently indent the middle of each round with a teaspoon to form a valley. Add ½ to 1 teaspoon of fruit preserves.

7. Bake for 12 minutes, until golden brown.

Apple Chocolate Cake

Recipe donated by Elena Arpino

SERVES 8

  2 cups flour
  ⅛ teaspoon salt
  1 teaspoon cinnamon
  1 teaspoon baking soda
  3 large apples
  ½ teaspoon lemon juice
  ¾ cup vegetable oil
  1 cup sugar
  2 eggs
  2 teaspoons vanilla
  ½ cup chopped walnuts
  ½ cup dark chocolate chunks or chips

1. Preheat oven to 325 degrees.

2. Sift together flour, salt, cinnamon, and baking soda in a medium mixing bowl; set aside.

3. Peel and core three large apples and thinly slice; sprinkle with lemon juice.

4. Combine vegetable oil, sugar, and eggs in a large mixing bowl; mix until creamy. Add vanilla, chopped walnuts, and chocolate chunks or chips; mix well. Slowly add flour mixture and combine until mixture becomes dough-like. Fold in apple slices with a heavy spatula.

5. Lightly coat the inside bottom and sides of a 10-inch loaf or tube pan with butter. Sprinkle flour into the pan and shake to completely cover the surface. Shake out all excess flour.

6. Pour the batter into the prepared loaf or tube pan. Bake for one hour or until a toothpick inserted into the middle comes out clean (not including any melted chocolate).

At a time in history when Boston was perceived as a place filled with racial disharmony, Elena Arpino and her fellow employees at Instrumentation Laboratories found a common bond that bridged the divide—food! Most women working in the factory between 1960 and 1970 were from Ireland, Italy, Poland, Russia, or the South. All came from very different backgrounds. They shared a special passion for their own style of cooking but had a great interest in seeing "how the other person made it." This recipe was a collaborative effort of all these ladies. Before and after work, and during lunch breaks, they chatted and developed the recipe. After a few trials and errors, the recipe evolved to the point at which everyone in the group was happy.

7. Remove cake from oven and cool in the pan for about one hour.

8. Once cooled, turn loaf upside down and tap out onto a serving plate.

Southern Sweet Potato Pie

Recipe donated by Massie Burch

~ SERVES 8

1 9-inch piecrust (see page 235)
2 large sweet potatoes, peeled and quartered
½ teaspoon nutmeg
1 cup sugar
¼ pound butter, softened
½ cup shredded coconut
⅛ teaspoon allspice
⅛ teaspoon lemon
2 tablespoons cream (optional)

1. Line the bottom of a 9-inch pie pan with the piecrust.

2. Place sweet potatoes in a medium saucepan with enough water to cover. Boil until tender.

3. Preheat oven to 400 degrees.

4. Combine sweet potatoes, nutmeg, sugar, butter, coconut, allspice, and lemon in a large mixing bowl; mix until creamy. If sweet potatoes were very fresh before being boiled, you may want to add approximately 2 tablespoons of cream to get a more creamy mixture.

5. Pour mixture into the piecrust. Bake for 45 minutes.

Sweet Potato Pie

Recipe donated by Angela Parris

SERVES 8

1	9-inch piecrust (see page 235)
6–8	medium-sized sweet potatoes
3	eggs, lightly beaten
1½	cups sugar
½	cup milk
1½	teaspoons vanilla
½	teaspoon cinnamon
½	teaspoon nutmeg
½	teaspoon ginger
½	teaspoon allspice
1	tablespoon butter, softened
6½	ounces evaporated milk

1. Line the bottom of a 9-inch pie pan with the piecrust.

2. Place sweet potatoes in a medium saucepan with enough water to cover; boil over high heat until soft. Drain water and allow sweet potatoes to cool. Peel skins; place sweet potato flesh in a medium mixing bowl and mash.

3. Preheat oven to 450 degrees.

4. Add eggs, sugar, milk, vanilla, cinnamon, nutmeg, ginger, allspice, and butter to the bowl with the mashed sweet potatoes. Mix well until smooth. Slowly stir in evaporated milk.

5. Place aluminum foil under the pie pan and bring up around the edges to cover the top diameter of the crust to prevent burning. Pour sweet potato mixture into piecrust.

6. Bake for 15 minutes at 450 degrees; reduce oven temperature to 350 degrees and bake for an additional 40 minutes. Pull down aluminum foil and bake for an additional 15 minutes.

7. Cool. Serve plain or with fresh whipped cream or ice cream.

Pound Cake

Recipe donated by Mabel Sanders
~ SERVES 10

    3 cups sugar
    1 pound butter, softened
    6 eggs, room temperature
    3 cups flour
    ½ cup milk
    1 tablespoon orange or vanilla flavoring

1. Preheat oven to 325 degrees.

2. Combine sugar and butter in a large mixing bowl; mix until creamy. Add eggs one at a time, mixing continuously.

3. Slowly add flour then milk to batter; mix well. Add orange or vanilla flavoring and mix until smooth.

4. Lightly grease the inside bottom and sides of a 12-cup Bundt pan with butter. Sprinkle flour into the pan and shake to completely cover the surface. Shake out all excess flour.

5. Pour batter into the pan. Bake for 1½ hours or until top is golden. Remove from oven and cool in pan for at least one hour. When cool, place a serving plate over the Bundt pan, turn over, and gently tap the cake out to serve.

Cousin Louise's Almond Pound Cake

Recipe donated by Eldora B. Lewis

SERVES 10

- 3 cups sugar
- ¾ pound butter, softened
- 9 eggs, room temperature
- 1 tablespoon almond flavoring
- 3 cups cake flour

1. Preheat oven to 350 degrees.

2. Combine sugar and butter in a large mixing bowl; mix until creamy. Add eggs and almond flavoring then slowly add flour; mix until smooth and creamy.

3. Lightly grease the inside bottom and sides of a 9-inch tube pan with butter. Sprinkle 2 tablespoons of flour into the pan and shake to completely cover the surface. Shake out all excess flour.

4. Pour batter into pan and bake for 1 hour and 15 minutes, or until tooth-pick inserted in center of cake comes out clean.

5. Remove from oven and allow to cool for one hour before serving.

Lemon Pound Cake

Recipe donated by Susan Davis
SERVES 10

- 2 cups confectioners' sugar
- 1 pound butter, softened
- 6 eggs, room temperature
- 3 cups self-rising flour, sifted
- 2 teaspoons lemon flavoring

1. Preheat oven to 325 degrees.

2. Combine sugar and butter in a large mixing bowl; mix on medium speed until creamy. Add eggs one at a time, mixing continuously. Slowly add flour and mix until fully incorporated. Add lemon flavoring and mix until thick but smooth.

3. Lightly coat the inside bottom and sides of a 12-cup Bundt pan with butter. Sprinkle flour into the pan and shake to completely cover the surface. Shake out all excess flour.

4. Pour batter into the pan. Bake for 45 minutes or until top is golden.

5. Remove from oven and allow to cool in pan for at least one hour. When cool, place serving plate over the Bundt pan, turn over, and gently tap out the cake to serve.

Southern Pound Cake

Recipe donated by Massie Burch
SERVES 10

5 eggs, room temperature
3 cups sugar
1 tablespoon vanilla
1 tablespoon lemon flavoring
¾ pound butter, softened
3 cups self-rising flour
1 cup milk

You may need to adjust the oven temperature a bit as the top may burn if the oven gets too hot. The oven temperature should be set to approximately 347 degrees. If the top does burn, it is fine to simply cut the burnt part off. This is a very dense cake, and takes tender loving care to make it perfect.

1. Preheat oven to 347 degrees and place oven racks six inches apart.

2. Combine eggs, sugar, vanilla, lemon flavoring, and butter in a large mixing bowl; mix until smooth. Add flour, one cup at a time, mixing well after each addition. Add milk and mix until fully incorporated.

3. Fill a large rectangular baking pan approximately three quarters of the way up with cold water. Place in the oven on the lower rack.

4. Pour batter into a greased angel food pan and place in the oven on the upper rack. Bake for 2½ hours without opening the oven door. After 2½ hours, check the cake and lower the oven temperature if necessary. The cake is done when the top is just dark golden.

5. Remove cake from the oven and set on a wire rack to cool. When cool, remove cake from pan and serve.

Spanish Cake

Recipe donated by Elizabeth Halfkenny

~~ SERVES 10 TO 12

5½ tablespoons butter, softened
1 cup sugar
2 eggs, room temperature, separated
½ cup milk
1¾ cups flour
3 teaspoons baking powder

1. Preheat oven to 350 degrees.

2. Combine butter, sugar, egg yolks, milk, flour, and baking powder in a large mixing bowl; mix until combined.

3. Beat egg whites until stiff in a medium mixing bowl; fold into batter and incorporate.

4. Lightly coat the inside bottom and sides of a 9-inch tube pan with butter. Sprinkle 2 tablespoons of flour into the pan and shake to completely cover the surface. Shake out all excess flour.

5. Pour batter into pan and bake for one hour or until toothpick inserted in the center of the cake comes out clean. Remove cake from oven and cool. When cool, remove from pan and serve.

French Cookies

Recipe donated by Frida Leyzerovich

✎ MAKES ABOUT 4 DOZEN COOKIES

These delicious cookies need extra care when handling the dough. Try your best to make even round balls. You may need to wipe your hands between rolling.

½ pound butter, softened
½ pound Ricotta or Mascarpone cheese
1 cup flour
¼ teaspoon salt
2 egg whites
1 cup sugar for sprinkling

1. Combine butter, cheese, flour, and salt in a large mixing bowl; mix until dough is an even texture. Cover and refrigerate dough for 2 hours.

2. Preheat oven to 450 degrees. Grease cookie sheets.

3. Beat 2 egg whites lightly in a small bowl; set aside. Place sugar in a separate small bowl; set aside.

4. Remove dough from refrigerator. Hand-roll one teaspoon of dough into a ball. Repeat until all dough is used. Dip tops of dough balls into egg whites then into the sugar. Place balls sugar-side up on cookie sheets.

5. Bake for approximately 10 to 12 minutes or until tops are rose-colored. Remove from oven. Cool cookies on paper towels.

Heidelberg Cake

Recipe donated by Myra Marino
SERVES 10

1	cup seedless raisins
1½	cups cold water
1½	teaspoons baking soda
2	cups sugar
3	eggs
1	cup vegetable oil
1	teaspoon vanilla
3	cups flour, sifted
1	teaspoon salt
1	cup chopped walnuts

1. Preheat oven to 375 degrees.

2. Bring raisins and water to a boil in a small saucepan. Add baking soda, stir, and set aside to cool.

3. Combine sugar, eggs, oil, and vanilla in a large mixing bowl; mix well. Add sifted flour and salt; mix well. Fold in raisin mixture and walnuts.

4. Grease a 10-inch tube pan or angel food pan. Pour batter into pan and bake for one hour. Remove from oven and cool. Remove cake from pan and serve.

Spice Cake

Recipe donated by Elizabeth Halfkenny

SERVES 10

- 2 cups sugar
- ½ cup butter, softened
- ½ cup processed lard or vegetable shortening
- ⅛ teaspoon salt
- 1 cup whole milk
- 2 cups flour
- 2 teaspoons baking powder
- 2 teaspoons cinnamon
- 1 teaspoon nutmeg
- 1 teaspoon allspice
- ½ teaspoon ginger
- 1 cup raisins
- ½ cup chopped pecans
- 3 egg whites, room temperature

1. Preheat oven to 350 degrees.

2. Combine sugar, butter, and lard or vegetable shortening in a large mixing bowl; mix until smooth. Add salt, milk, flour, baking powder, cinnamon, nutmeg, allspice, ginger, raisins, and pecans; mix well.

3. Beat egg whites until stiff in a medium mixing bowl. Fold into batter and incorporate.

4. Lightly grease the inside bottom and sides of a 10-inch tube pan or 12-cup bundt pan with butter. Sprinkle flour into the pan and shake to completely cover the surface. Shake out all excess flour.

5. Pour batter into pan. Bake for one hour. Remove cake and allow to cool before serving.

Saint Petersburg Pie

Recipe donated by Larisa Polyak

❧ SERVES 8

      7 ounces butter, softened
    ¼ cup sour cream
      1 large egg
      1 cup sugar
    2½ teaspoons baking powder
      2 cups flour
    1½ cups rhubarb, cubed
      1 apple, peeled, cored, and cubed
      4 plums, pitted and cubed
      3 tablespoons fresh cranberries

This recipe has been in my family for well over 100 years. When this pie was made, it was a sure sign that spring had arrived. Be creative in placing the dough squares on top of the pie, but be sure to allow a few spaces for air to escape. Use early spring rhubarb that is fresh and young for best taste. If it is later in the season and spring rhubarb is unavailable, sprinkle approximately one tablespoon of sugar over the rhubarb cubes. You may need to bake for an additional 10 to 15 minutes if using summer rhubarb.

1. Combine butter, sour cream, egg, sugar, baking powder, and 1½ cups of flour in a large mixing bowl. Mix and knead well.

2. Divide dough into two even sections. Roll out one section on a lightly floured work surface.

3. Grease a 9-inch pie pan. Place the rolled-out dough into the pan, making sure it is evenly spread on the bottom and sides. Cut off any excess dough. Mix rhubarb, apple, plums, and cranberries. Add to pie shell.

4. Preheat oven to 500 degrees.

5. Add remaining ½ cup flour to the second section of the dough. Mix and knead well. Roll out on a flat work surface and cut into ¾-inch squares. Place the dough squares over the fruit filling, placed sporadically or in a circular pattern. Pinch together any pastry that meets around the edges of the pie.

6. Bake pie for 5 minutes. Reduce heat to 350 degrees and bake for 20 minutes, or 35 minutes if using summer rhubarb. Reduce heat again to 120 degrees and bake for an additional 15 minutes. Remove from oven and set aside to cool.

Coconut Cake

Recipe donated by Massie Burch
❧ SERVES 8 TO 10

- 3 eggs
- ¼ pound butter, softened
- 2 cups sugar
- 3 cups self-rising flour
- 1 cup milk
- 1 teaspoon vanilla

Filling:
- 2½ cups shredded coconut (you may substitute drained, crushed pineapple)
- 1 cup sugar
- ¼ pound butter

Phyllis Kaplowitz, executive chef of Jacob Wirth & Co., is pictured above with Sheila Burch, a server there for 17 years, and her mother, Massie. At one time, Jacob Wirth, one of Boston's oldest restaurants, did not allow women in the main dining room. This was a normal practice at the time throughout the country. It's great to see these three ladies talking about food in the main dining room at Jacob Wirth, and to realize how much times have changed.

1. Preheat oven to 350 degrees.

2. Combine eggs, ¼ pound butter, and 2 cups sugar in a large mixing bowl; mix until creamy. Slowly add flour, milk, and vanilla; mix thoroughly.

3. Lightly grease the inside bottoms and sides of three 8-inch round baking pans with butter. Sprinkle flour into each pan and shake to completely cover the surface. Shake out all excess flour.

4. Divide batter evenly between the three pans and bake for 40 to 45 minutes or until a toothpick inserted into the center comes out clean. Remove cakes from oven and set aside to cool.

5. Combine coconut (or pineapple), 1 cup sugar, ¼ pound butter, and 1¾ cups water in a medium saucepan. Bring to a boil over high heat. Reduce heat and simmer for 25 minutes; set aside to cool.

6. Remove cakes from pans. Place first layer on a cake plate and top with the filling. Top with the second layer and frost again. Repeat with the third layer.

Banana Cake

Recipe donated by Sally Landowski
❧ SERVES 12

2/3 cup vegetable shortening

1½ cups sugar

2 eggs, room temperature

1 cup ripe to over-ripe mashed bananas

½ cup sour milk (or ½ tablespoon vinegar with enough milk added
to make ½ cup)

2 cups flour

1 teaspoon baking soda

½ cup chopped walnuts

1. Preheat oven to 350 degrees.

2. Combine shortening and sugar in a large mixing bowl; mix until creamy. Add eggs one at a time, mixing well after each addition. Add mashed bananas and mix until combined.

3. Sift together flour and baking soda. Alternate adding sour milk and flour with baking soda to batter; mix well. Fold in nuts.

4. Grease a 9 by 13-inch baking pan or 10-inch tube pan. Pour in batter. Bake for 30 minutes or until toothpick inserted into the center comes out clean.

5. Remove from oven and allow to cool. Cake may be served plain or frost with a vanilla buttercream frosting.

Banana Cake with Chocolate Bits

Recipe donated by Tonny Wong

 SERVES 12

 ¼ pound butter, softened
1¼ cups sugar
 2 eggs, room temperature
 2 ripe bananas, peeled and mashed
 ½ cup sour cream
 2 cups flour
 1 teaspoon baking powder
 1 teaspoon baking soda
 ⅛ teaspoon salt
 1 teaspoon vanilla
 ¾ cup semisweet chocolate morsels

1. Preheat oven to 350 degrees.

2. Combine butter and sugar in a large mixing bowl; cream until smooth. Add eggs and mix well. Fold in mashed bananas. Sift together flour, baking powder, baking soda, and salt. Slowly mix flour mixture into batter. Add vanilla and sour cream and fold in chocolate morsels.

3. Lightly grease the inside bottom and sides of a 9 by 13-inch baking pan with butter. Pour flour into the pan and shake to completely cover the surface. Shake out all excess flour.

4. Pour batter into the baking pan. Bake for 35 minutes or until a toothpick inserted in the center comes out clean. Remove from oven and cool before serving.

Jimmy Cake

Recipe donated by Sally Landowski
SERVES 10 TO 12

- ½ cup vegetable shortening
- 2 cups confectioners' sugar
- 4 eggs, room temperature, separated
- 2 cups flour
- 2 teaspoons baking powder
- 1 cup milk
- 1 cup multicolored jimmies or sprinkles
- 2 cups chopped walnuts

1. Preheat oven to 350 degrees.

2. Place shortening in a large mixing bowl and gradually add sugar, mixing until creamy. Beat egg yolks and add to shortening mixture; mix well.

3. Sift flour with baking powder over a small mixing bowl. Repeat process three times.

4. Alternate adding milk and the flour mixture to the shortening and sugar mixture; mix well. Add jimmies and nuts. Mix until incorporated.

5. Beat egg whites until stiff. Fold into cake batter. Pour batter into a 9 by 13-inch baking pan or 10-inch tube pan. Bake for 30 minutes or until toothpick inserted into the center comes out clean.

6. Remove from oven and allow to cool. Top with a vanilla or buttercream frosting and sprinkle with additional jimmies.

Italian Date Cookies

Recipe donated by Antonia LiDonni

MAKES ABOUT 8 DOZEN COOKIES

- 2 cups sour cream
- 10 cups flour
- 4 eggs, room temperature
- 3 cups sugar
- 1 pound butter, softened
- 2 teaspoons baking soda
- 4 teaspoons baking powder
- 2 cups fresh chopped dates
- 1 cup confectioners' sugar

This recipe has been in my family for over four generations. I learned it from my aunts who lived in Santa Elia, Italy, which is a small mountain village right outside of Monte Casino. You may freeze logs after baking. Allow to cool then wrap well. Thaw completely before slicing as needed. These cookies have the texture of soft biscotti.

1. Combine sour cream, 3 cups flour, eggs, sugar, butter, baking soda, and baking powder in a large mixing bowl; mix until smooth. Fold in chopped dates. Gradually add the remaining flour; mix well.

2. Preheat oven to 350 degrees.

3. Place a large handful of dough on a large floured work surface and hand roll into a log approximately 2½ inches in diameter by 10 inches long. Repeat making logs until all dough is used.

4. Place two dough logs at a time on an ungreased cookie sheet. With hand cupped thumb to pinkie, lightly roll and press on the tops of the logs to make a slight indentation approximately every 2 inches along the logs.

5. Bake for 18 to 20 minutes. Remove from oven to cool.

6. When cool, cut each log at 30 degree angles and dust cookies lightly with confectioners' sugar to serve.

Banana Cream Pie

Recipe donated by Dale Mitchell
 SERVES 8

      1 9-inch piecrust (see page 235)
     ⅓ cup flour
     ⅔ cup sugar
     ⅛ teaspoon salt
      2 cups milk
      2 egg yolks, lightly beaten
      2 tablespoons butter
      1 teaspoon vanilla
      2 ripe bananas

Meringue:
     ¼ teaspoon salt
     ¼ teaspoon vanilla
      2 egg whites
      6 tablespoons sugar

1. Preheat oven to 350 degrees.

2. Line the bottom of a 9-inch pie pan with the piecrust. Partially bake piecrust for approximately 5 minutes. Remove from oven and set aside.

3. Combine flour, sugar, and salt in a medium mixing bowl; mix thoroughly. Scald milk in a medium saucepan or double boiler over medium heat. When milk is just about to boil, reduce heat to low and gradually add flour mixture, stirring constantly. Simmer over very low heat, stirring often, for approximately 5 minutes, or until thick and custard-like.

4. Lightly beat egg yolks in a small bowl. Add approximately ⅓ cup of the hot custard mixture and mix well. Pour mixture back into the custard and stir well. Add butter. Stir and cook for 2 minutes over low heat. Stir in vanilla. Remove from heat and set aside to cool.

My mother sent me her secret Banana Cream Pie recipe in 1973 when I was first starting out in Boston. Not having much money, this dessert was great to bring to the potluck suppers that were so popular at the time. Now, as executive director of Ethos, a sister agency to Central Boston Elder Services, I still enjoy and appreciate making this delicious pie.

6. Make make the meringue, combine salt, vanilla, and egg whites in a medium mixing bowl. Beat to a stiff foam. Add 1 tablespoon of sugar at a time until egg whites form stiff peaks.

7. Peel and slice bananas into prebaked piecrust and cover with custard mixture. Spread meringue evenly on top and bake for approximately 15 minutes. Remove from oven and cool before serving.

Homemade Donuts

Recipe donated by Jim Poutre

MAKES ABOUT 3½ DOZEN

1¾	teaspoons salt
4	teaspoons baking powder
2	teaspoons nutmeg
1½	teaspoons ginger
3½–4	cups flour, sifted
1¾	cups sugar
1	tablespoon vegetable shortening
2	egg yolks
2	whole eggs
2	cups sour buttermilk (sour the milk with 2 tablespoons vinegar or let it sour on its own)
2	teaspoons baking soda
4	cups oil, lard, or vegetable shortening for frying

This is my grandmother's recipe. Her name is Ruth Austin. As a kid, I remember watching her making these over her cast iron skillet. She would use her special two-prong fork to gently turn the donuts. These will always be my original comfort food. The trick to making these donuts is to always roll out half the batter and return remaining pieces to bowl until all the dough is used. Otherwise, the batter dries out and the last donuts fried will be tough. Donuts may be served plain or coated in confectioners' sugar or white sugar.

1. Combine salt, baking powder, nutmeg, ginger, and flour in a medium bowl; set aside.

2. Combine sugar, shortening, egg yolks, and eggs in a large mixing bowl; mix until creamy. Add sour buttermilk and baking soda, then slowly add flour mixture. Mix and knead well.

3. Heat oil to 370 to 380 degrees in a large stockpot.

4. Take half the batter and roll it out on a lightly floured work surface. Cut out donuts with a well-floured cutter. Return cuttings and donut holes to bowl with batter. Repeat process until all batter is used for donuts.

5. Carefully place donuts into hot oil with spatula and fry on one side for 1 to 1½ minutes. Turn donuts over with a fork and cook other side for approximately 1 minute. Lift from oil with fork, being careful not to prick. Place donuts on brown paper to cool.

6. Serve plain or sprinkle with sugar or confectioners' sugar.

Best Needhams

This is a delicious Christmas gift I've made for years! Cake paraffin is the same paraffin used to make jelly.

Recipe donated by Judy Montgomery

MAKES 5 DOZEN

- 3 large potatoes, peeled and quartered
- ½ teaspoon salt
- ¼ pound margarine
- 7½ cups confectioners' sugar (2 pound package)
- 2⅔ cups flaked coconut
- 2 teaspoons vanilla

Chocolate Dip:
- ½ cake paraffin (2½ inches by 2½ inches)
- 1½ cups chocolate bits
- 4 squares unsweetened chocolate

1. Place potatoes in a medium saucepan with enough water to cover. Bring to a boil over high heat and cook until tender, approximately 20 minutes. Drain well. Add salt and mash. This should yield approximately ¾ cup mashed potatoes. Set aside.

2. Melt margarine in the top of a double boiler over boiling water. Add mashed potatoes, confectioners' sugar, flaked coconut, and vanilla; mix well. Turn mixture into a greased 15 by 10-inch jelly-roll pan; spread evenly and set in a cool place to harden.

3. Make chocolate dip in a double boiler by melting paraffin over boiling water. Add both chocolates and allow to melt, mixing well.

4. When potato mixture is hard, cut into small 1-inch squares. Place a toothpick in the middle of each square and dip into the chocolate mixture. Hold squares above chocolate mixture after dipping so they drain well; place on wax paper to harden.

Paczki

Recipe donated by Louise Kinoske
☙ MAKES ABOUT 30 DONUTS

12 egg yolks
 1 teaspoon salt
 2 packets dry yeast
¼ cup 110 degree water
 1 cup heavy whipping cream
⅓ cup butter, softened
½ cup sugar
 4 cups flour
 3 tablespoons dark rum
 3 tablespoons grated orange peel
 8 ounces black cherry or blueberry preserves
 6 cups vegetable oil
 2 cups sugar for coating

1. Combine egg yolks and salt in a medium mixing bowl. Mix at high speed until thick. Set aside.

2. Dissolve dry yeast in ¼ cup 110 degree water and set aside.

3. Scald whipping cream in a small saucepan over medium heat. Remove from heat and set aside to cool to lukewarm temperature.

4. Combine butter and sugar in a large mixing bowl; mix until creamy. Add yeast mixture.

5. Slowly add 2 cups flour to the lukewarm cream, mixing constantly. Add rum, orange peel, and the remaining 2 cups flour. Add egg yolk mixture and knead well until all air bubbles disappear and dough comes clean from hands.

6. Cover with a clean cloth and let dough sit in a warm place until it doubles in size, approximately one hour. Punch dough down and let it rise again to double in size.

In Poland, Paczki is the traditional "Fat Tuesday" or Mardi Gras celebratory treat. Cooking fats and oils are forbidden during Lent so this is a good way to use up all extra fats before Ash Wednesday. This recipe is ambitious, but it is well worth the time and effort. These taste best when fried in lard, but vegetable oil or a combination will also work fine.

7. Roll dough out to approximately ¼ inch thick on a floured work surface. Lightly sprinkle flour on top of dough. Cut dough into rounds with the rim of a 2-inch glass or cookie cutter. Top half the rounds with approximately ½ teaspoon fruit preserves. Top with remaining rounds and pinch together edges to form a very tight seal. If dough is dry, moisten edges with a sprinkle of water before pinching together.

8. Lightly roll between palms to form balls. Place donuts on a floured board, cover, and let sit until doubled in size.

9. Heat oil in a deep fryer or stockpot to 360 to 370 degrees. Carefully drop a few donuts at a time into the oil and fry for approximately 5 to 6 minutes or until golden brown all around. Remove from oil with a slotted spoon and set on absorbent brown paper or paper towels to drain and cool. If oil gets too hot while frying, drop slices of a cool, peeled potato into oil to reduce temperature and burnt taste.

10. Once donuts are cool, roll evenly in sugar and serve.

Index